WORKING IN TEAMS
A Team Member Guidebook

Sandy Pokras

A FIFTY-MINUTE™ SERIES BOOK

CRISP PUBLICATIONS, INC.
Menlo Park, California

WORKING IN TEAMS
A Team Member Guidebook

Sandy Pokras

CREDITS
Managing Editor: **Kathleen Barcos**
Editor: **Regina Preciado**
Typesetting: **ExecuStaff**
Cover Design: **Carol Harris**
Artwork: **Ralph Mapson**

Copyright © 1997 Viability Group Inc.

Printed in the United States of America by Bawden Printing Company.

Distribution to the U.S. Trade:

National Book Network, Inc.
4720 Boston Way
Lanham, MD 20706
1-800-462-6420

Library of Congress Catalog Card Number 96-86712
Pokras, Sandy
Working in Teams
ISBN 1-56052-412-X

10 9 8 7 6 5 4 3 2 1

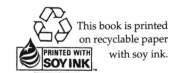
This book is printed on recyclable paper with soy ink.

LEARNING OBJECTIVES FOR:

WORKING IN TEAMS

The objectives for *Working in Teams* are listed below. They have been developed to guide you, the reader, to the core issues covered in this book.

Objectives

❑ 1) **To explain the mechanics of organizing teams**

❑ 2) **To discuss the roles of individuals in teams**

❑ 3) **To present procedural strategies for successful team work**

Assessing Your Progress

In addition to the Learning Objectives, Crisp, Inc. has developed an **assessment** that covers the fundamental information presented in this book. A twenty-five item, multiple choice/true-false questionnaire allows the reader to evaluate his or her comprehension of the subject matter. An answer sheet with a summary matching the questions to the listed objectives is also available. To learn how to obtain a copy of this assessment please call: **1-800-442-7477** and ask to speak with a Customer Service Representative.

ABOUT THE AUTHOR

Sandy Pokras is president of Viability Group, Inc., a team building, communication training and management consulting firm in Northern California since 1973. His training workshops teach team managers, leaders, facilitators and members to achieve high-performance teamwork.

As a corporate consultant, program designer, keynote speaker, and conference facilitator, Mr. Pokras conducts sessions for a wide range of organizations, including IBM, Chevron, Federal Reserve Bank, Westinghouse, Siemens, University of California and the U.S. Postal Service.

Mr. Pokras is the author of numerous management articles as well as *Rapid Team Deployment* and *Team Problem Solving,* published by Crisp Publications in 1991.

ABOUT THE SERIES

With over 200 titles in print, the acclaimed Crisp 50-Minute™ series presents self-paced learning at its easiest and best. These comprehensive self-study books for business or personal use are filled with exercises, activities, assessments, and case studies that capture your interest and increase your understanding.

Other Crisp products, based on the 50-Minute books, are available in a variety of learning style formats for both individual and group study, including audio, video, CD-ROM, and computer-based training.

CONTENTS

INTRODUCTION: WHAT'S TEAMWORK ALL ABOUT?

Webster's Dictionary says that a team is:

Two or more horses harnessed to the same plow.

Maybe that's why some people get the idea that teams exploit them, stress them, and squeeze them. But if things go right, the opposite happens.

Why do organizations form teams? Your department might want to get people from different groups together to solve a problem. Maybe the competition is doing better so you need to improve how you do things. Or maybe your manager wants to develop the combined brainpower of all coworkers. Whatever the reason, teams can benefit both the company and you—if you do them right!

The definition of a good team is:

A group of willing and trained individuals who are . . .

- united around a challenging common goal,

- structured to work together,

- sharing responsibility for their task,

- depending on each other, and

- empowered to implement consensus decisions.

The type of project doesn't matter. Your group becomes a team when you all get involved, briefed, trained, and prepared, and then you accept the challenge.

It helps to have an official team assignment because you'll be able to take time away from your other duties. Your team has a much greater chance of success when you need each other to succeed. When you and your teammates decide that you're all for one and one for all, you'll start working closely together. You'll feel like the owners of your own little business inside the big business. If you're given the power to act on what you decide, you'll know what high-performance teamwork can be.

P A R T

I

Direction

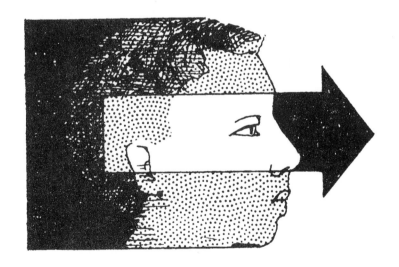

TEAM DIRECTION

Before you commit to a team, you need to know what's expected of you and how your participation will affect your current job. To contribute effectively, you need to see the big picture. What do the customers need? What is the history of the problem? When you first hear about a new team, ask about its mission statement, which means: The special assignment, role, or function of the team, usually expressed as a short statement of purpose that defines the scope of the problem, the boundaries of the process, and the needs of the team's customers.

Here's the first episode of our imaginary team that you will follow through the steps outlined in this book:

CASE STUDY: Storm Rebuilding Team

Chris works for Public Service, Inc., a company that does building projects for the city. Every spring Chris and her coworkers are assigned to rebuild curbs and sidewalks after intense winter storms. After a few seasons of grousing about doing the same kind of work over and over and wasting taxpayer money, Chris decided to form a team to do something about it.

When Chris approached Terry, PSI's project manager, the obvious question was "What would this storm rebuilding team do?" Chris presented a rough mission statement:

Find a way to prevent winter storms from doing the same damage to curbs, sidewalks, and parks every year.

Terry talked with Fran, the city's public works director, who seemed to like the idea. After recruiting a small group of city and PSI employees and managers to join the Storm Rebuilding Team, Fran, Terry and Chris got everyone together to talk about the idea. Chris's rough mission statement was good enough to get everyone interested.

EMPOWERMENT

Before teams, most people had to choose between going along with their bosses (even when the bosses were wrong) or speaking up and being labeled a troublemaker. Teams provide safety in numbers.

We call delegating power and giving decision-making authority to employees close to the work *empowerment*. It should include:

- Getting you to own and buy into the team's mission,

- Giving you some influence and control over your own work,

- Making you responsible for implementing your decisions, and

- Holding you accountable for what you do.

You already know that, in the real world, empowerment isn't absolute. Your team might be called self-directed but others still have something to say about your work. It's more accurate to say that you'll share some power with other managers or departments.

Team Power

Others' Power

Teamwork can help you learn, grow, and stand out. It might benefit your job, your career, and even your attitude. But there's also a risk. Do you think this team can succeed? Check into what your options are and what the consequences will be. Will participation be worth it? What might you gain? You might not have a choice at the outset, but by doing your homework at least you'll know how to work with your team for the best chance of success.

EXERCISE: *Personal Decision*

Consider your personal goals and decide if you believe the team experience will help you personally. When you're ready, answer these questions.

1. TEAM MISSION: What is the mission statement of the team?

_____

_____

_____

_____

2. EMPOWERMENT: How much power will this team have?

_____

_____

_____

_____

3. PERSONAL GOALS: What's in it for you?

_____

_____

_____

_____

4. DECISION: Will you agree to join or at least see how it goes at first?

_____

_____

_____

_____

13 Qualities of High-Performance Teams

QUALITY	DESCRIPTION
Purpose	A clear, challenging, and inspiring common purpose defined
Membership	Complete, willing, skilled, available, and trained membership
Leadership	Leadership with high standards that builds the team and guides results until the team takes charge
Structure	A flexible, fully-defined, results-oriented structure of roles, processes, and procedures under team control
Plans	Long-range master plans and short-range action plans based on an appropriate team road map with measurable milestones
Participation	Active participation of all team members who pull their fair share and follow through
Communication	Open communication channels, active listening, and fully informed members
Trust	Mutual trust, support, and collaboration so that teammates back up each other
Consensus	Critical decisions by consensus especially when differences produce conflict
Ownership	Joint ownership and shared responsibility for implementation
Synergy	High synergy, meaning total team energy is greater than the sum of its individual parts
Recognition	Appropriate rewards, frequent recognition, and routine celebrations
Empowerment	Sufficient empowerment with active external support enabling the team to achieve its mission

TEAM LIFE CYCLE

The best way to build teams is to follow the phases of *a Team Life Cycle*. First, define *team direction* with a mission statement. This starts with someone getting the idea for the team approved, deciding that the investment will be worth the costs, and taking the lead in forming it.

Establish *team organization* starts when you're asked to join. Before you get too deeply involved, make sure you and your new teammates have the resources necessary to success. Work out a team charter, a written agreement of how you'll operate and what you'll be responsible for, and a master plan, a timeline of milestones of when you hope to accomplish what.

Begin *team building*, growing good chemistry, while you're forming, when you get to know each other and learn to work together. It's like inventing a new alloy by combining separate metals into one unique material. During training you'll set up ground rules, decide who'll do what, and learn to make joint decisions.

You'll make real progress on your assignment when you reach the *teamwork* phase. You'll talk to people outside meetings, run some experiments, meet frequently, present your findings, disagree and decide by consensus. No matter how well things go, you will want to practice *continuous improvement*. At this stage you'll review the team's progress, get feedback, improve your work, troubleshoot obstacles, and help each other.

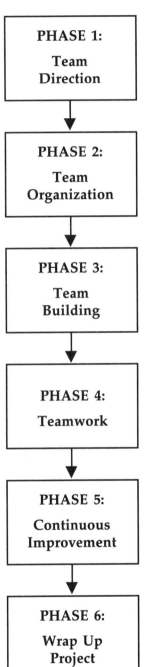

PHASE 1:
Team Direction

PHASE 2:
Team Organization

PHASE 3:
Team Building

PHASE 4:
Teamwork

PHASE 5:
Continuous Improvement

PHASE 6:
Wrap Up Project

TEAM LIFE CYCLE (continued)

Some teams go on forever. If your project reaches an end point, you'll need to conclude properly. *Wrap up project* includes evaluating your results, documenting your findings, reporting to your sponsor, communicating what you learned, celebrating, and recognizing those who contributed.

We'll discuss each of these phases in detail. To help you make sense of the team process, we'll follow an imaginary team as it goes through each of the steps outlined in this book. You will also find individual and team exercises that will help you apply each concept to your own situation.

INDIVIDUAL VS. TEAM WORK

Good teamwork depends on working with others and helping them do their part. Cooperation becomes all important. To oil the wheels of a team, you need to understand, get along with, and respect your teammates. Good team members cover for and support each other without being asked. This is a major change for people who've spent their lives looking out for number one and doing things their own way.

In a sense, we're talking about the difference between owning your own business and having a partner.

Spending time and effort building working partnerships will improve team chemistry. Team chemistry has three parts: communication, consensus, and contracting. We'll discuss communication throughout this whole book, especially when we study supporting teamwork and achieving consensus. Right now we need to look at getting closer to your teammates and developing agreements with them, which we call *contracting*.

Getting Closer To Your Teammates

Teamwork requires that you get to know your teammates' work history, skills, and personality. Plan to visit each other's work areas and talk about your current job and work history. If you pay attention, you'll learn a lot about each other during training and team meetings. You might even have the luxury of a team-building retreat dedicated to building relationships.

INDIVIDUAL VS. TEAM WORK (continued)

Don't expect to work on a team where everybody is totally compatible. Packing a team with different personality types opens minds through natural controversy. Your team might deliberately include representatives from conflicting groups to force you to look at things from many different angles. Inheriting a few inbred conflicts that others haven't been able to resolve can be interesting unless it gets personal. How do you avoid that?

One way is to approach each other according to your *social styles*. Social style means someone's personality type, main approach to others, and common behavior patterns.

People who concentrate on . . .	Tend to . . .
Results	Drive self and others to quick, tangible, and measurable results.
Accuracy	Always be thinking, analyzing forces, and considering events.
Interaction	Communicate ideas and feelings openly and expressively.
Harmony	Act agreeable, supportive, and cooperative, and smooth feelings.

Each style has value and is necessary for effective teamwork. Of course, people are more complex than any one type. We all have strengths and weaknesses from each category that change from situation to situation. As you work with your new teammates, you'll begin to identify their style preferences.

Aim to understand your teammates' styles. Do this by approaching each person according to what they prefer. Give straight answers to a results-oriented person, reveal your underlying thinking to an accuracy-driven teammate, listen and openly express your thoughts and emotions with an interactive person, and be extra concerned about politeness and positiveness with a harmony-driven teammate.

EXERCISE: Social Styles

Once you meet your teammates and work with them for a while, fill out the following form to identify how to best relate to them.

Teammate	Preferred Style	Backup Styles	Best Approach
You			

CONTRACTING

Because you have to volunteer for teamv
when a boss or coworker orders you to
your willingness and commitment. Most
buy-in by making sure that you do impo
We also use the term *contract*, which is:
members or supporters to do something
until renegotiated.

If you don't take commitments seriously,
renegotiate whenever you need to.

Examples of Contracts

What contracts do you need? Some exam

- Commitment to join the team,

- What roles you'll play,

- How you'll support other members (your partners), and

- What actions you'll do for the team.

Some group contracts you'll create are:

- Mission statement,

- Team charter,

- Master plan, and

- Team ground rules.

The *Personal Decision Exercise* earlier asked you to decide what's in it for you
if you join the team. Combining your commitment with others is a good
example of a contract. Most people only commit when they see a personal
benefit in what's required. If you personally value the team assignment, then
you're more likely to accept its goals, communicate openly, feel ownership,
and support your teammates.

How To Develop Contracts

To develop group contracts, it's not enough to just *think* about your level of commitment. Invest the time to talk together about wants and needs. Good teams get explicit about what they expect. You'll make faster progress if you each listen to and respect everyone else's position. Team members who run off and take action without others' buy-in aren't very popular. That's why it's important when forming teams to focus on mission, ground rules, charter, plans, and roles. See that your team first contracts with yourselves and then get your bosses to contract too.

What Are Ground Rules?

One of the most important contracts for a forming team to work on is *team ground rules.* These are a list of phrases or short sentences that members agree on defining how they want to operate and treat each other.

Ground rules describe things like how you should behave, communicate, treat each other, prepare for and run meetings, make decisions, solve problems, and resolve conflicts. Good ground rules are clear, consistent, agreed to, reinforced (not enforced or policed), and followed.

When your team starts, discuss and define the most obvious ground rules at your first meeting. Don't expect to cover every conceivable issue. Just publish the list and post it on a chart for use during all meetings. Follow them and encourage everyone else to do the same. As you progress, you'll probably revise your ground rules or develop new ones for new situations.

CASE STUDY: *Team Ground Rules*

Here is the Storm Rebuilding Team's initial list.

- Come to all meetings on time and be prepared.

- Leave your rank outside the room.

- Respect what other team members say.

- When you disagree, hear someone out, present your views, and then try to find a solution.

- Complete your action assignments on time.

- If you must miss a meeting or can't complete an action item, tell the team leader in time to get someone to cover for you.

- Read meeting minutes when you receive them, ideally within 24 hours following each meeting.

Unconscious guidelines like these might develop naturally over time. Unfortunately, unconscious patterns don't help you and your teammates to get along and complete your work fast enough. So talk about ground rules, agree on them, post them, follow them, and refine them.

EXERCISE: *Ground Rules*

Fill out the following Ground Rule Worksheet so you'll be ready to
contribute suggestions about how you think your new team will operate.

How will we . . .

Work together?

_____

_____

Establish plans?

_____

_____

Make work assignments and set schedules?

_____

_____

Monitor and follow up on work assignments?

_____

_____

Keep each other fully informed?

_____

_____

Give feedback to each other?

_____

_____

EXERCISE: Ground Rules (continued)

Recognize accomplishment?

_____

_____

Organize and conduct our meetings?

_____

_____

Ensure that everyone participates fully?

_____

_____

Make decisions?

_____

_____

Resolve differences and solve problems?

_____

_____

Make the best use of limited resources?

_____

_____

Ensure that we achieve desired results?

_____

_____

PART

II

Organization

THE TEAM CHARTER

After you've been briefed by your team sponsor, you'll want to develop a team charter. A *team charter* is a clear, written, agreed-upon description of the team's mission and how it relates to the organization's goals. It includes the authority, resources, and key mechanics necessary to achieve its mission and it serves as a contract between team members and between the team and its sponsor. A good one will:

► Give you all the same clear sense of direction.

► Show you how the team's work fits in to the rest of the organization.

► Help you understand what's expected of you—and what's not.

► Provide a clear picture of your boundaries, limits, and constraints.

What Goes In It?

Each component of a team charter answers specific questions about the team's direction, membership and empowerment. Here are some samples of what to consider as you define your general direction, membership requirements, and empowerment.

General Direction
- Background
- Mission
- Road Map Choice
- Deliverables
- Name

Empowerment
- Authority Level
- Resources
- Team Metrics
- Reporting
- Recognition and Rewards

Membership
- Customer Requirements
- Stakeholders
- Team Member Roles
- Team Duties
- Team Sponsor Role

CASE STUDY: *Developing a Team Charter*

Most teams don't work out every team charter component at the start of their work, but the Storm Rebuilding Team did.

GENERAL DIRECTION	
Background	Every winter, storms ravage city streets, curbs, and parks, causing considerable damage. Chris, a lead worker at PSI, suggested to Terry, PSI's project manager, that some of the repeating problems could be fixed once and for all.
Mission	Find a way to prevent winter storms from doing the same damage to curbs, sidewalks, and parks every year.
Road Map Choice	Problem-solving.
Deliverables	• Report compiled from city records showing which repairs have been repeated most often and what they cost, within two months. • Completed field tests by midsummer proving which frequently damaged areas can be permanently fixed and which aren't worth it. • Complete permanent repairs before the first winter freeze.
Name	Storm Rebuilding Team
MEMBERSHIP	
Customer Requirements	• Residents want safe, usable streets, sidewalks, and parks. • Taxpayers want minimum cost. • City officials need laws and regulations followed.

Other Stakeholders	• County Public Works Department • State Department of Transportation • City Auditors Office • City employees • PSI management, shareholders and employees
Team Member's Roles	• Chris, Pat, Loren, all PSI employees • Mary, assistant city engineer • Dale, city purchasing rep • Sal, city accounting clerk • Jan, city building inspector • Terry, PSI project manager = team leader • Fran, city Public Works Director = team sponsor • Ray, city trainer = team facilitator
Team Duties	• 1–2 hours weekly: team meeting • 2–5 hours weekly: collect data, meet stakeholders, conduct tests, and troubleshoot problems • Monthly: informal progress report • As needed: document findings, make presentations, oversee repairs
Team Sponsor's Role	Provide full briefing and access to information, ongoing guidance, timely feedback on proposals, action on roadblocks, serving as team champion, troubleshooting conflicting priorities of team members' managers

CASE STUDY (continued)

EMPOWERMENT	
Authority Level	• Without requesting team sponsor approval, the team can: —Collect data from PSI and city records —Contact city and PSI employees and suppliers —Design and run tests to find and solve problems —Manage its own budget • The team should request team sponsor approval for: —Changes that significantly impact the city's master plan or contracts with PSI —Modifications to supplier relationships —Recommendations that contain risk to the public —Expenditures that exceed the team's budget
Resources	• Team members' time commitment: approximately 10 percent • Training: Team Kick-Off Workshop, team facilitator just-in-time sessions, quarterly retreats, other as needed • Technical support: available through normal channels • Supplies: team notebook, team kit, flipchart • Budget: $17,500
Team Metrics	• Days ahead or behind team master plan • Team budget • Repair costs calculated the next spring

Reporting	• Weekly meeting minutes to team sponsor • Biweekly team sponsor/team leader one-on-one meetings • Monthly team sponsor informal progress presentation • Milestone completion presentations to customers and stakeholders
Recognition & Rewards	• Free meal tickets at the end of each road map step • $100 bonus for completing major deliverables on time • Team member input to individual performance reviews • All contributors to team success will receive choice follow-up assignments to further their careers

You've already read about contracts, so you realize that a team charter is a two-way street. Your management briefs you and lets you figure out the details. You decide what you plan to do, and then your team sponsor approves it. Everyone honors your team charter until you decide to change it (see page 24). Treat yours as a living document. Review it every now and then and update it when needed.

EXERCISE: Team Charter Priorities

Here's an exercise to help your new team to develop its charter.

▶ Make sure you understand each part of a team charter.

▶ Decide how important you think each item will be for your new team.

▶ Using the list of team charter components, label each item:

M = must agree right away

C = can work on later

N = not real important

_____ Background	_____ Team Duties
_____ Mission	_____ Team Sponsor Role
_____ Road Map Choice	_____ Authority Level
_____ Deliverables	_____ Resources
_____ Name	_____ Team Metrics
_____ Customer Requirements	_____ Reporting
_____ Stakeholders	_____ Recognition & Rewards
_____ Team Member Roles	

TEAM CHARTERS

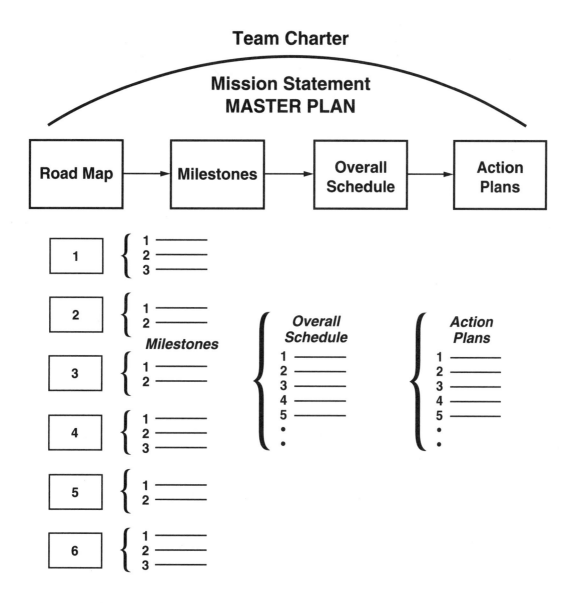

Team Charter

Mission Statement
MASTER PLAN

| Road Map | → | Milestones | → | Overall Schedule | → | Action Plans |

The *team charter* is the umbrella that will give you a general sense of direction so together you can focus on your assignment. One of its most important pieces is the team's mission statement.

A charter may give you strategy and structure, but you need to work out plans to decide what you'll do and when.

MASTER PLANS

A *master plan* is an overview of the most important results that your team intends to accomplish. It includes: A *road map,* to outline the step-by-step route your team will follow; *milestones,* the specific, measurable targets your team decides upon as checkpoints along the way; an *overall schedule,* to provide a target start and finish date for each milestone and road map step; and *action plans,* which are the individual steps you and your teammates will take to reach each milestone.

Once you've developed your master plan, try to follow it without jumping ahead or getting sidetracked. Do everything possible to stay on course.

How to Develop Master Plans

Follow these four steps to develop a master plan.

1. Choose the road map that best fits your team's mission and deliverables. If none of them fits, make up your own. (See page 29 for road map samples.)

2. Brainstorm outcomes needed to accomplish each road map step.

3. Evaluate the list, prioritize your deliverables and select one to three SMART (**S**pecific, **M**easurable, **A**greed-to, **R**esult-orient and **T**ime-bound) milestones for each road map step.

4. Establish an overall schedule by juggling milestone timeframes against team charter deliverables.

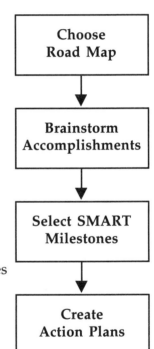

Rewrite your plan into one clear document and map out a project-tracking diagram.

CASE STUDY: *Team Master Plan*

Remember the deliverables in the Storm Rebuilding Team's charter?

► Report compiled from city records of which repairs have been repeated most often and what they cost, within two months.

► Completed field tests before the end of summer proving which damage areas can be permanently fixed and which aren't worth it.

► Completed permanent repairs before the first winter freeze.

Their master plan includes these major results plus smaller milestones arranged around the problem-solving road map.

ROAD MAP STEPS	MILESTONES
Organize and Plan	• Recruit and train team members this week. • Hold first meetings next week to establish ground rules. • Agree on team charter and master plan within two weeks.
Describe Problem	• Publish a report compiled from city records listing which repairs have been repeated most often and what they cost, within two months.
Identify Root Cause	• Work with experts to decide how to test frequently damaged areas before the end of month three. • Complete field tests by midsummer proving which areas can be fixed permanently and which can't.
Decide Solution	• Decide how to fix chosen areas by August 1. • Complete drawings and get approval by August 31.
Implement Corrective Action	• Work out building plans, logistics, resources, and task assignments before beginning work. • Complete permanent repairs before the winter freeze.
Improve System	• Monitor how things work during the winter. • Publish a report summarizing progress by the middle of spring, including suggestions for further improvements.
Wrap Up	• Decide whether to recharter the team by July 1. • Hold an early July awards dinner to celebrate success. • Review, recognize, and reward team members by July 31.

ROAD MAPS

Different kinds of teams need different approaches. The road map* you choose will tell you the best way to get where you want to go. Following a road map ensures that you don't forget any critical actions. They lay out the preferred order of the key steps that similar teams took to reach their goal. The right road map provides a tested method that ensures even first-time teams won't omit essential actions.

With a logical order of approaching the assignment defined in advance, a team can plan and act quickly. Road maps carve up seemingly overwhelming tasks into more manageable chunks, provide milestones, suggest tools to use, and make it easier to hold teams accountable for results without too much stress.

There are seven common road map types, from the simple task road map to the complex steering council road map. A brief description of each road map follows.

---

*For more in-depth information about specific roadmaps, read *Rapid Team Deployment* by Sandy Pokras. Menlo Park, CA: Crisp Publications. 1995.

Road Map Types

TYPE	PURPOSE	KEY ACTIONS
Task	Implement a well-defined, specific short-term action	1. Contract 2. Plan 3. Do 4. Check 5. Next step 6. Final report
Problem Solving	Eradicate an undesirable, unpredictable, or unworkable situation	1. Organize and plan 2. Describe problem 3. Identify root cause 4. Decide solution 5. Implement corrective action 6. Improve system 7. Wrap-up
Process Reengineering	Streamline a working but inefficient process	1. Organize and plan 2. Define requirements 3. Flowchart process 4. Monitor process 5. Make improvements 6. Standardize improvements 7. Wrap-up
Process Control	Improve results and better control a specific stable process	1. Organize and plan 2. Define customer satisfaction 3. Describe current process 4. Identify process measurements 5. Measure current process 6. Improve process 7. Assess progress 8. Wrap-up

ROADMAP TYPES (continued)

TYPE	PURPOSE	KEY ACTIONS
New Product or Process	Develop and introduce a new product or new process	1. Organize and plan 2. Concept 3. Requirements 4. Design 5. Development 6. Testing 7. Implementation 8. Maintenance 9. Wrap-up
Natural Work Group	Improve a continuing job by working together better	1. Organize and plan 2. Define customer satisfaction 3. Define processes 4. Partner with suppliers 5. Systematize production 6. Measure performance 7. Charter projects 8. Continuously improve
Steering Council	Define direction, establish structure, and coordinate	1. Organize and plan 2. Direction 3. Data collection 4. Change plans 5. Structure 6. Resource definition 7. Communication system 8. Recognition and reward system 9. Continuous improvement

Brainstorm Accomplishments

Once you've developed a road map, resist the temptation to jump right into action. Take some time to brainstorm outcomes needed to accomplish each road map step. When your brainstorming winds down, come back and evaluate what you've listed, surface priority accomplishments, and select one to three to serve as milestones for each step. Follow these brainstorming guidelines:

Clear Question

Clearly announce the focus of the brainstorming session. Post the exact question on a flipchart.

Suggest Ideas

Contribute whatever ideas come to mind, striving for quantity, not quality. Cover all wild and crazy viewpoints. Include everyone.

Accept Everything

Accept all ideas, however impractical or crazy. Listen and acknowledge. Post all answers using the speaker's words. Use multiple recorders if needed to keep up.

No Editing

Don't edit, criticize, or evaluate any suggestion. Discussing ideas isn't brainstorming! You'll have time to clarify later.

Build On

Let comments trigger new thoughts. If you react to an idea, volunteer different ones instead of judging or editing.

SMART MILESTONES

Choose one to three accomplishments for each road map step to serve as your milestones. Make them SMART with this worksheet.

Accomplishment: What do you want the team to achieve?
Specific: What do you want to accomplish?
Measureable: How will you monitor progress?
Agreed-Upon: How will this milestone satisfy each team member's needs?
Result: What is the finished product or final outcome?
Time-Bound: How long will it take to complete this milestone?
MILESTONE: Rewrite the milestone to include all the above.

ACTION PLANNING

An action plan defines your tactics. It is:

*A complete series of steps in the order
necessary to accomplish a milestone.*

When you're ready to start a road map step or big milestone, spend a meeting figuring out what actions are needed and who will be responsible. The best action plans include who does what, by when, and in what order. Sometimes resources, standards, measurements, or reporting are added as well.

CASE STUDY: Action Plan

The Storm Rebuilding Team's second road map step was to publish a report compiled from city records of which repairs have been repeated most often and what they cost, within two months. This is the action plan they developed.

WHO	ROLE	WHAT	BY WHEN
Chris	PSI employee	Review PSI records for repeated repairs	May 7
Mary	Assistant city engineer	Review city records for repeated repairs	May 7
Pat	PSI employee	Compile a list of repeated repairs	May 15
Terry	Team leader	Convene team meeting to review findings	May 20
Dale	Team leader	Circulate minutes of meeting for review	May 25
Sal	City accountant	Look up costs	June 5
Jan	City building inspector	Review data against building permits for accuracy	June 10
Fran	Team sponsor	Meet with team to discuss findings	June 15
Dale	Team recorder	Publish report	June 30

ESTABLISH OVERALL SCHEDULE

Now that you have SMART milestones for each road map step, you need to create an overall schedule. Look at the time required for each accomplishment and the master deadlines in your team charter. Juggle one against the other and adjust milestones to ensure your work will be completed on time. A Gantt chart is a helpful tool.

How To Draw a Gantt Chart

Gantt charts were first used in the early 1900s by an engineer named Henry Gantt. He drew horizontal bars that graphically show the starting and ending points of each major step of a project. To create one, name the earliest action at the top left of the chart (where it says 2.1.1) and list later actions below (2.1.2 to 2.1.7). Label the timeline at the bottom with days, weeks, or months and write a date by each hashmark. Then draw bars next to each step, beginning at the start time and finishing at the end time according to the timeline. The resulting chart visually displays the flow of activities and can also show simultaneous steps.

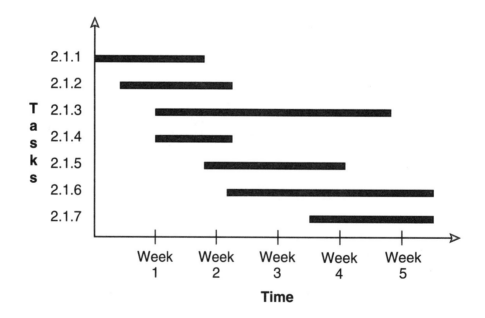

For more details about project planning and management see Marion E. Haynes, *Project Management: From Idea to Implementation,* Crisp Publications, Inc. 1996.

TEAM SUPPORT ROLES

Because teams don't work in a vacuum, you can't expect success without outside support. The following chart and definitions explain the structure that most high-performance teams use to provide leadership, guidance, and outside help.

Structure of a High Performance Team

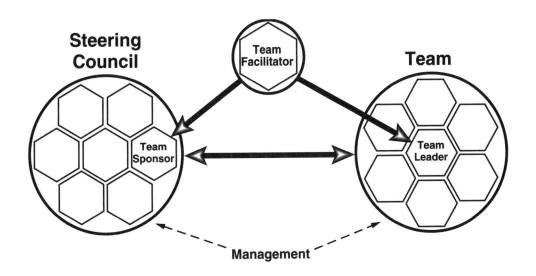

TEAM SUPPORT ROLES (continued)

Definition of Roles

ROLE	WHO	RESPONSIBILITIES
Team Leader	Elected or appointed team member who builds the team and guides joint action on its work or project	Build the team by initially conducting meetings, coordinating teamwork, coaching team members, following-through on plans, guiding outside contacts, and delegating to the team
Team Sponsor	Manager who owns the territory or mentor who is delegated responsibility for the team problem or process, and champions its work	Initiate the team by staffing and briefing, negotiate the team charter, provide direction and guidance, authorize time and resources, monitor progress, give timely feedback, hold team accountable, plus promote, support, and remove barriers
Team Facilitator	Team process expert outside the chain of command, assigned to help the team but not to serve as a member	Guide team set-up, provide team training, coach team leader, help build the team sponsor about its dynamics, growth, and problems
Steering Council	A model team of team sponsors or their bosses who coordinate and guide the team environment	Establish vision, develop strategic plans, organize training, define processes, charter teams, monitor progress, publicize results, and provide rewards

CASE STUDY: *Team Support Roles*

Team Leader: PSI's management discussed in depth who should lead the Storm Rebuilding Team. Terry, PSI's project manager, was chosen initially because of experience in building other teams. Terry agreed to turn the job over to Chris, who promoted the idea initially, or to whoever the team preferred after a few months.

Team Sponsor: It didn't take much discussion to decide who should serve as team sponsor. Fran, the city's Public Works Director, already controls the purse strings and naturally fills this role.

Team Facilitator: Ray, the city's trainer, was asked to facilitate the team due to his several years of related experience.

Steering Council: After discussion, it was clear that no existing body—PSI's board or the city council—had complete enough representation to oversee the team's work. Fran and Terry recruited PSI's CEO, a city council member, two department heads, a park supervisor, and a vocal community group leader to meet monthly to guide the team's work.

EXERCISE: *Support Roles*

Fill out the following worksheet to select your nominations for your new team's leadership and support roles and to identify key functions.

ROLE	WHAT DOES THE TEAM NEED FROM EACH?	WHO SHOULD DO IT?
Steering Council	_____	_____
	_____	
Team Sponsor	_____	_____
	_____	
Team Facilitator	_____	_____
	_____	
Team Leader	_____	_____
	_____	

SELECTING YOUR TEAM LEADER

Webster defines *leader* as "the horse harnessed at the front of the team." A better definition of team leader is:

> *A member who takes the first step when things need to be done, gets the team to follow, and eventually turns all power over to the team. It's a dual role: guiding joint action on the team's work while building team chemistry until the team is self-sufficient.*

Often, management appoints an experienced team leader at first. That's fine as long as one leader balances team growth with work results. Otherwise the team may never grow up and learn to share the leadership functions it needs to operate at a high level. High-performance teams either let their appointed leader remain a figurehead while they go about their business, or they rotate the function every few months to give everyone some practice.

Team Leader Functions

Whether right at the start or after some time, pick your team leader wisely. Choose someone who thinks one or more steps ahead, communicates well, and cares about you, your teammates, and your overall work, as well as themselves. Choose someone who would be good at these five roles:

- Building your team

- Coaching team members individually

- Coordinating team efforts

- Chairing meetings

- Organizing outside contacts

TEAM MEMBER'S ROLES

As a team member you should be an active player. Politeness is good, silence when you have opinions and feelings isn't. You'll be most active when you have a stake in the team's success. This could happen if your main job depends on the team's success or if your boss explained why your participation is important. Either way, being a team member includes:

► Willingly sharing responsibility for the team's work,

► Conducting experiments and collecting input before team meetings,

► Contributing information and expertise during meetings, and

► Representing the team to customers, suppliers, and coworkers.

Effective team members are vocal, open, and honest. They listen, support, and cooperate. They stay involved in all aspects of the team's work, and pull their fair share.

Follow Through on Commitments

Keeping commitments may be the most important responsibility of team members. If you accept an action assignment and don't follow through, the next meeting could become a waste of time. If others get into the same habit, your team will see little or no progress. Here are some suggestions about how to follow through on your commitments.

► Only accept assignments you have the time and know-how to complete.

► If you want to contribute but have conflicting priorities, negotiate with your boss to get outside support.

► Set up a personal reminder system so you don't forget.

► If you run into a problem, ask for help from your leader or a teammate.

► If something prevents you from keeping a commitment, hand off the assignment to a teammate who can finish it.

► Don't surprise the team with an incomplete action item.

TEAM MEMBERS' MAIN FUNCTIONS	
Support the Team	• Help define charter, plans, ground rules, and action steps • Follow the team's road map, plans, and ground rules • Understand team roles and take responsibilities seriously • Get to know other team members and cooperate fully • Help resolve team problems and internal differences
Represent the Team	• Make frequent personal contacts with stakeholders • Keep outsiders informed about team progress • Contribute to written reports • Actively participate in team presentations
Support the Team	• Review team meeting minutes • Complete actions and follow-through commitments on time • Collect input and gather information about team proposals • Meet with team leader or other members as needed • Prepare to participate fully and be on time for all meetings
Represent the Team	• Offer special knowledge and expertise • Think creatively and use brainstorming tools • Communicate, listen openly, and help build consensus • Recognize others' contributions and encourage feedback

TEAM MEMBERS' ROLES (continued)

Team Functions

As you're forming, your team might have trouble adjusting to doing things together. Once you've figured out your charter and plans, though, it becomes clear how much there is to do. You'll realize quickly that you need each other. Instead of everyone doing everything, high performance teams divide tasks, trust each other to follow through, and share the workload.

A good way to share the load is to create dedicated roles, and refer all similar issues to an internal expert. These mini-leaders guide the whole team in their areas of specialty.

If you need to crunch some numbers, select a team accountant who's good with math. If your project requires technical work, appoint a skilled member to take the lead. If you have unpopular duties like housekeeping, set up a rotation. Remember, the mini-leader just leads in getting the task done. Everyone should volunteer to assist and back up.

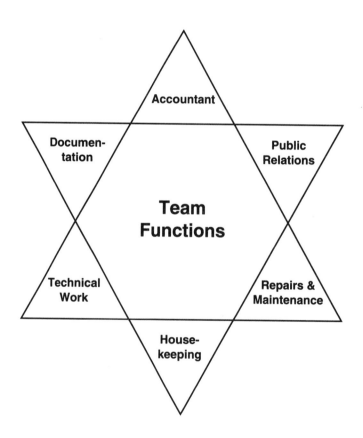

Team Workshops

Two team workshops can help you figure out these assignments. The *Role Workshop* is a retreat or long meeting dedicated to choosing roles. The *Expectations Workshop* works better when you already have defined roles and want to get clearer on how you can better support each other.

Role Workshop

Use this workshop to analyze your team assignment, distribute task responsibilities, and clarify the roles you'll each play.

STEP	EXAMPLE
List the skills and expertise that the team's work requires.	*Number-crunching, making visual aids, interviewing senior executives.*
Group these talents together in functional packages with similar requirements.	*Team statistician, team artist, equipment specialist.*
Consider which team members' jobs require them to give special attention to which of these functions.	*As a supervisor, Terry is concerned with preventive maintenance.*
Consider which team members have experience, demonstrate flair, or express interest in these skills.	*Mary is good with people, Fran always wanted to learn computer graphics.*
Assign functional specialties to team members equally so that everyone pulls their weight.	*Pat = team record keeper, Chris = technical adviser.*

TEAM MEMBERS' ROLES (continued)

Expectations Workshop

Use this workshop to determine what you and your teammates expect of each other, resulting in everyone agreeing on how each of you can best contribute to the team.

STEP	EXAMPLE
Write down what you think the team expects you personally to contribute using the first row (where it says "me") on the **Expectations Worksheet**.	*Be prepared and on time for meetings and share experience when it relates*
Fill in your teammates' names below *teammates*. To the right of each one, write what you expect them to contribute to the team.	*Chris = be serious and helpful.* *Pat = open up and give more details.*
When preparations are complete, the discussion moderator asks volunteers to present what they wrote in the first row, explaining what they think the team expects of them.	*Be prepared and on time to meetings and share experience when it relates*
After hearing one member's answer, the discussion moderator should ask others to explain what they wrote after each teammate's name. Identify similarities and reach consensus where expectations are different.	*Most of us agree that experience is valuable but I could give it with fewer words* *Everyone likes Chris's playful mood but use fewer tangents*

EXERCISE: Expectations Worksheet

Me	What I think the team expects me to contribute
Teammates	What I expect each teammate to contribute

Your Public Relations Role

When your team solves a problem or improves a work process, you'll probably want to change the way some procedures are done. You know that change is hard on some people. That's why an essential part of teamwork is to prepare outsiders for change. You do this by working closely with people outside the team relaying their feedback to the team, and selling them on your proposals. You will need to communicate with anyone outside the team who will be affected by the changes your team wishes to implement. Typically called stakeholders, this group includes internal and external customers and suppliers, coworkers later in your production flow, managers who depend on your work output, those with veto power, and anyone else whose help you need or who is affected by what you do.

TEAM MEMBERS' ROLES (continued)

Your team's public relations work starts by identifying your stakeholders. Then you assign various audiences to specific team members to stay in touch. Group and assign them sensibly. For example, put the sales manager on your team in charge of all contact with sales and marketing stakeholders.

This chart shows you and your teammates at the center as the core team. The second ring, consultants, are part time or occasional contributors who need to be in touch with what the core team is doing. The outside ring represents those with whom you will rarely meet; but who have a big stake in your team's accomplishments.

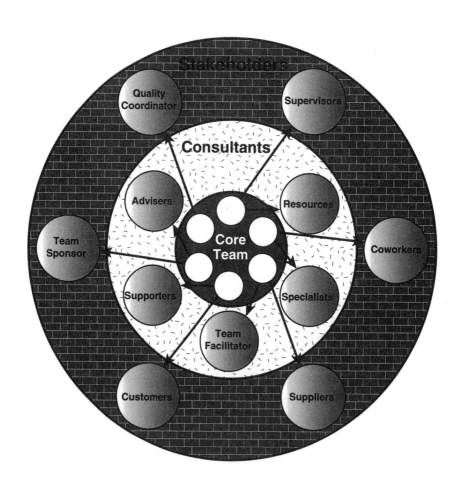

Maintain regular contact and meet individually with anyone you've agreed to represent. Maybe you can influence these parties to support the team and maybe you can't. Your primary mission is to keep the lines of communication open for these three reasons.

Three Reasons for Contact

Getting Input

- Gathering data

- Surfacing new viewpoints about a problem

- Suggesting solutions to problems created by team changes

Informing

- Keeping others updated about team progress

- Checking in with stakeholders about interim findings

- Warning customers and suppliers about unpopular decisions

Gaining Support

- Identifying supporters and soliciting resources

- Pre-selling before presentations

- Winning support of those with veto power

CASE STUDY: Team Member Roles

Here are the roles and responsibilities that the storm rebuilding team set up.

Team Member	Regular Job Function	Delegated Team Responsibilities	Stakeholder Representation
Chris	PSI crew member	PSI records	PSI crews
Pat	PSI crew member	Team historian	State & federal parks
Loren	PSI crew member	Public Relations organizer	Community groups
Mary	Assistant city engineer	City records	PSI & City engineering
Dale	City purchasing rep	Team minutes	Other cities and counties
Sal	City accounting clerk	Team accountant	Regulatory agencies
Jan	City building inspector	Team planner	Suppliers & vendors
Terry	PSI project manager	Team leader	PSI management
Fran	City public works director	Team sponsor	City manager, city council
Ray	City trainer	Team facilitator	City, PSI human resources

EXERCISE: *Team Member Roles*

► List the members of your new team and their existing jobs.

► Based on what you each do, suggest what team roles might be a good fit to delegate to each member.

► Based on the preferences you think your team members have, suggest which stakeholders each should contact.

TEAM MEMBER	REGULAR JOB FUNCTION	DELEGATED TEAM RESPONSIBILITIES	STAKEHOLDER REPRESENTATION

P A R T

III

Working Together

BUILD YOUR TEAM

Hopefully by this time your team has developed some positive chemistry. If you survived the forming stage of development, you and your teammates:

- ► Know each other enough to build working relationships,

- ► Are informed and have discovered your goals and direction,

- ► Have a picture of your roles and responsibilities,

- ► Decided to commit to the effort, and

- ► Are clear that you each can make a valuable contribution.

If you've found enough common ground by developing charters, plans, and ground rules, you should begin to feel comfortable, needed, and respected. But not every team bonds quickly, permanently, or solidly enough.

Face it: there's more to teamwork than just facts and figures, charters and plans. The human element is vital to your success. You need to routinely make time to work on your team chemistry.

When your team has made plans and is willing to talk, you've passed the forming stage. Your reward is storming: tension, friction, and sometimes conflict. Storming is natural. If you take it in stride and learn to adjust to each other, you'll discover that conflict can be constructive. In fact, learning to manage conflict is essential to reaching high performance.

BUILD YOUR TEAM (continued)

Maybe the best advice for accepting storming is to focus on problems, not people. That's easier said than done when a teammate argues with your pet proposal or puts you down. Welcoming storming is certainly an acquired taste. You can speed the journey by:

Cultivating Participation

► Let your teammates talk and be themselves

► Encourage them to share their feelings and reveal hidden agendas

► Build mutual trust by allowing them to vent

► Recognize and learn to adjust to different social styles

Resolving Differences

► Welcome and identify conflicts as early as possible

► Confront and work through differences

► Resolve power and other issues as they occur

► Always try to negotiate win-win solutions

To function well together as a team, you must learn to give each other constructive feedback and to work toward, and reach, consensus.

FEEDBACK

Feedback means one teammate's reaction to another's actions or statements. Healthy teams learn to communicate their reactions quickly and constructively. They negotiate until everyone is happy, and then hold each other accountable for the agreements made.

Forming teams don't give much feedback, especially when things go wrong. Let's say, for example, you agree on ground rules, plans, or action items. Something unexpected gets in the way, and you don't follow through as promised. Because you're still forming, little is brought up in public. But you can bet some members are grousing to each other in private.

When you reach the storming stage, your team will open up more, even if it isn't with a helpful attitude. For example, if you miss an action item, you'll hear about it. This is progress. It can be painful, but it's still progress.

In the beginning, you may want your leader or facilitator to give all the feedback. While this helps short-term comfort, it's better for all of you to struggle with the learning process. When you have the confidence to handle whatever comes up, storming will be a distant, nonthreatening memory.

When to Give Feedback

You might find yourselves giving feedback in situations when teammates:

- Don't seem to understand

- Take discussions off track

- Do things that are helpful to the team

- Show attitudes that make you uncomfortable

- Behave in a way you think disrupts or hurts the team

- Use language you object to

- Change for the better

- Violate some ground rules

- Aren't opening up because authority figures are present

- Dominate discussion or grandstand and the team isn't interested.

FEEDBACK (continued)

Sometimes it's better one-on-one and sometimes it's better with the whole group. An example of one-on-one feedback would be telling a teammate privately that a meeting was a waste because he didn't complete an action item. An example of whole-team feedback would be pointing out that many team members are late with action items. Then the group can deal with the bigger issue together. Neither method is fun, because people tend to react. But feedback gets easier as team relationships improve.

One-On-One Feedback

Let's look in more detail at the two kinds of one-on-one feedback recommended for teamwork: positive reinforcement and advice. Researchers estimate that most children receive 35 times more negative feedback than positive while growing up. To counteract this conditioning, teams should use 80 percent reinforcement and only 20 percent advice.

You do this by acknowledging, encouraging, praising, agreeing, and siding with your teammates. Place a checkmark by any methods below that you plan to use.

- ☐ A friendly, smiling, interested attitude

- ☐ Catching someone doing something right

- ☐ Expressing confidence in a teammate's ability

- ☐ Frequent one word acknowledgments like *good*, *right*, or *fine*

- ☐ Verbal praise when someone solves a problem

- ☐ Personal compliments about a teammate's strengths

- ☐ Compliments for asking good questions

- ☐ Concerned questions to find out how the person is doing

- ☐ Accepting your teammate's input and suggestions

Positive Reinforcement Guidelines

Here are some suggestions about how to give positive reinforcement . . .

Encouragement   Your purpose is to encourage a specific action, behavior, or performance so that it will be repeated.

Pure   Mixing reinforcement with criticism or advice dilutes it and may poison the desired effect.

Positive   Your aim is to reinforce what you want, so concentrate on the positive and ignore undesirable actions.

Value   Expressing the value of the person's actions must genuinely acknowledge them to be effective.

Support   Your feedback should support what people are trying to accomplish or what they are having difficulty with.

Specific Action   Recognize a specific event or behavior because general compliments tend to be taken as empty praise.

Descriptive   Your feedback should describe in detail what worked, what you liked, and why it was good.

Understandable   What you say should be clear, without unfamiliar technical terms or buzzwords.

Genuine   Use genuine statements, not canned phrases the same way over and over, or your sincerity will be questioned.

Immediate   Try to catch people doing something right, because reinforcement is strongest within 30 minutes after action.

Frequent   Positive feedback following each performance helps at first until the behavior is routine.

Reduce Later   Once your recognition is accepted, gradually reduce the amount you give so teammates don't become dependent.

FEEDBACK (continued)

Advice Guidelines

Even if you use all of the reinforcement techniques suggested, you still need to fix, change, adjust, and improve things. Here are some similar guidelines about how to give teammates advice.

Receptivity	Make sure your teammate is ready and willing to receive advice.
Descriptive	Your feedback should describe in detail how things are being done and how you think they should be changed.
Results	Back up your advice with proven results, actual reports, testimonials, or statistics.
Suggestions	Whenever possible, couch your advice as a suggestion, not as a *must* or a *should*.
Manageable Chunk	Give only a small amount of advice on one subject at a time.
Balance	Mixing advice with encouragement or compliments sometimes reinforces that you're honestly trying to help.
Positive	Ensure that you show that you really believe that your advice will help the person and team improve.
Tone	Keep your tone positive and avoid using a critical attitude or talking down to the person.
Just-In-Time	Give your advice just before the action is to occur so your teammate can practice right away.
Feedback	Ask for comments and reaction at any time to allow for clarification and keep communication open.

How To Accept Feedback

Just because you use constructive feedback doesn't mean that advice like this is easy to accept. Here are some ideas about how to accept advice.

- Listen carefully and try to see things from the other's point of view
- Breathe deeply and stay calm
- Clarify using questions to make sure you understand
- Acknowledge what you hear and understand without arguing
- Sort out what you've heard and decide what you agree with

Respond only after you've completed the above steps.

EXERCISE: 10 Feedback Examples

Here's an exercise to bring these guidelines closer to home.

▶ Mark which of these 10 examples of feedback are reinforcement (R) and which are advice (A).

▶ Which of the ones you marked follows the previous guidelines?

▶ How could you change any that don't follow the guidelines to be more constructive?

_____ **1.** Excellent team player

_____ **2.** No ability to work as a team member

_____ **3.** Very thorough on all tasks

_____ **4.** Needs to improve her attitude

_____ **5.** Always ahead of incoming work

_____ **6.** Should express feelings more openly to fix problems

_____ **7.** Poisons the team's mood with nasty comments

_____ **8.** Wears strange clothes

_____ **9.** I like working with her because she's cooperative

_____ **10.** Often gets defensive

FEEDBACK (continued)

Whole Team Feedback

Ultimately, you need to be up-front about feedback in a group setting. To do this well, be constructive, fair, honest, specific, and ongoing.

DO	DON'T
CONSTRUCTIVE	*DESTRUCTIVE*
• Help each other learn and grow • Suggest actions to take	• Put downs and bashing • Ganging up or hatchet jobs
FAIR	*NEGATIVE*
• Be objective and impartial	• Whining and complaining
HONEST	*JUDGEMENTAL*
• Be assertive and get your point across • Use actual observations of work	• Off-the-wall comments • Blanket generalities
SPECIFIC	*FILTERED*
• Give concrete, meaningful details • Back up with supporting examples	• Hidden agenda • Reluctant, holding back
ONGOING	*SURPRISING*
• Communicate openly • Give interim feedback	• Out-of-the-blue knee-jerks • Sudden overreaction

EXERCISE: *Whole Team Feedback*

Here's a feedback worksheet designed to help you better understand each other's needs and wants. To use it, get together with your team and give each other feedback on your relationships in this way.

▶ Privately fill out the following Feedback Worksheet about your teammates, making sure you apply the preceding guidelines.

▶ One team member at a time volunteers to receive feedback.

▶ The volunteer's teammates read what they wrote about him or her, carefully following the feedback guidelines. Be sure to give more positive feedback than advice.

▶ The volunteer summarizes any points and key issues that came up more than once. Record these summaries on a flipchart.

▶ If team and volunteer achieved better mutual understanding, wrap up here. If not, continue by discussing adjustments and action plans until the team and volunteer willingly contract to follow through.

Feedback Worksheet

Teammate	Continue Doing	Do More Of	Do Less Of	Start Doing

HANDLING DIFFERENCES

Being human, team members are naturally different. Many teams are purposely recruited with built-in differences in the hope that team members will work them out. As a result, tension within teams is expected. Most gradually overcome these frictions and become productive. But if team members focus solely on *"What's in it for me?"* instead of *"What's in it for the team?,"* progress gets slowed down.

Conflicts are critical forks in a team's path. Maturing teams learn how to work through or around personal needs without undermining the team. This often stimulates creativity and opens stagnant minds. On the other hand, inexperienced teams sometimes make things worse by ignoring situations until they blow up. They may label those who speak up as "nonteam players" and treat them as second-class citizens, which turns things personal.

The following flowchart shows how poorly handled differences turn into disruptions. If the team doesn't handle the disruptions according to the previous feedback guidelines, conflict can result.

- Backgrounds, education, and upbringing
- Values, beliefs, and philosophies
- Personal styles and preferences
- Job priorities and department objectives
- Individual ambitions

Differences
The natural diversity of the people who make up the team and the unique functions they represent

- Action items not completed
- Ground rules not being followed
- Domination, deference, and little cooperation
- Unwillingness to share workload
- Criticism and negative feedback

Disruptions
People feel friction and discomfort: the team gets distracted, wastes time, and gets off track

- Built-up tensions finally explode
- Nonstop venting and dramatizing
- Meetings out of control
- Team members quit or don't show up
- Permanent damage to relationships

Conflict
Complete communication breakdown with emotions out of control

CONFLICT RESOLUTION PRINCIPLES

You don't want to fall headlong into a complete communication breakdown with flaring tempers. But if you find your team slipping toward the cliff, follow these principles.

STEP 1: Welcome Differences

- ▶ Find something positive in every divergent view.

- ▶ Incorporate all statements into team discussion.

- ▶ Document all comments on flipcharts.

- ▶ Recognize, don't avoid, frustrated team members.

STEP 2: React Positively

- ▶ Create a safe place for team members to air differences.

- ▶ Keep a positive attitude in the face of conflict.

- ▶ Demonstrate belief in teamwork by always being constructive.

- ▶ Patiently but assertively moderate discussion, including venting.

STEP 3: Use Empathy

- ▶ Listen visibly, actively, and as an ally.

- ▶ Ensure everyone feels that their voice is heard.

- ▶ Consciously focus on the ideas and feelings of others.

- ▶ Try to see things from others' point of view.

CONFLICT RESOLUTION (continued)

STEP 4: Use Positive Feedback

► Use recognition and advice and "I" statements.

► Focus on the situation, not the person.

► Coach by being direct, specific, assertive, firm, and helpful.

► Use accepting body language to show clearly that others count.

► Balance everything you do with sincere positive reinforcement.

STEP 5: Confront Problems

► Explore differences by discussing all sides openly.

► Find root causes, not symptoms, to find permanent solutions.

► Take personal responsibility whether it's your problem or not.

► Turn all conflict situations into learning opportunities.

STEP 6: Negotiate Solutions Together

► Negotiate win-win using collaboration.

► Use ground rules to find joint answers.

► Use team's creativity to brainstorm alternatives.

► Facilitate group decision-making by seeking consensus.

► Build ownership by letting the team solve its own problems.

Win-Win Negotiating

The only negotiating style that works effectively in a team is win-win. You need to focus more on common interests than on personal gains. You're looking for solutions to joint problems and lasting agreements that all of you will take seriously. You need to agree instead of argue, cooperate instead of compete, and solve each other's problems instead of selfishly looking out for number one. If you succeed in negotiating a win-win solution out of a conflict situation, you'll increase commitment, reduce bad feelings, and prevent long-term grudges.

Here are four win-win methods with actions designed to replace competitive or contrary bargaining.

METHOD	DO	DON'T
Build Working Relationships	• Seek common ground • Separate people from problems	• Search for weakness • Look for advantages • Attack opponents
Explore Options for Mutual Gain	• Openly lay out needs • Share information	• Bargain, haggle, and horsetrade • Make concessions
Satisfy Both Sets of Interests	• Consider objective merits • Base decisions on principle	• Employ leverage • Base actions on manipulation
Solve Each Other's Problems	• Use wide-open creative thinking	• Limit thinking, dig in, close your mind • Use ultimatums

CONFLICT RESOLUTION (continued)

Win-Win Negotiating Agenda

To make win-win negotiation work, you need to assert your own point of view and reveal what's on your mind. You need to encourage the other side to do the same by questioning, listening, and discussing. Only then can you defuse your conflict, deal directly with issues, and use reason to arrive at solutions everyone can buy. Don't posture, distort, or hold back. Don't demand, pressure, or manipulate. And don't threaten, make wrong, or attack. Instead, follow these four steps, ensuring that your recorder captures everything on flipcharts and your discussion moderator keeps things on track.

Present

One at a time, present your reality completely while the others listen, acknowledge, and interrupt only to clarify understanding.

Agree

Together, find, discuss, and list areas of agreement, common goals, interests, values, and views.

Disagree

As the discussion progresses, identify key issues of disagreement that keep coming up or interferring with agreement. Narrow your key differences to the top one or two, discuss them in depth to understand each other's views, and define the exact problem.

Negotiate

Discuss and explore potential ways to resolve your differences, each trying to solve the other's problem in a way you can each live with. Consider and evaluate all of your options until you find a mutually acceptable solution for each issue. Then agree on steps needed to make it work.

EXERCISE: Conflict Resolution

Let's assume that the one-on-one advice you gave one of your new team members backfired. What would you do if the teammate got upset and blamed you for the problem? Using the principles of conflict resolution and win-win negotiating, craft an approach to resolve the situation. Record what you would actually say.

Present _____

_____

_____

_____

Agree _____

_____

_____

_____

Disagree _____

_____

_____

_____

Negotiate _____

_____

_____

_____

HOW TO RUN TEAM MEETINGS

Does this sound familiar? You get a memo to attend a meeting, but don't know why. You show up on time and wait around for a few latecomers. Discussion finally starts and you soon run out of time. People begin to leave before anything is concluded.

The bad news about teamwork is that you'll spend lots of time in meetings. The good news is with just a little work, you can make your meetings rapid and effective. Here are a few tools that can help.

Meeting Agendas

Meetings without agendas are like playing Russian Roulette. You might have a great discussion or you might wander off in a dangerous direction. It's best to keep the focus of each agenda on just one or two major themes so that all the pieces fit together. Good agendas include:

Starting time	When you hope to begin discussion on a topic
Presenter	Which member or guest will present or moderate
Topic	A word or phrase that identifies the subject for discussion
Process	The method or tool you'll use for the topic

CASE STUDY: Storm Rebuilding Agenda

START TIME	PRESENTER	TOPIC	PROCESS
		Opening	
3:34	Terry	Call to order, introductions, hats, icebreaker, minutes, update, agenda	Present and discuss
		Agenda Items	
4:00	Fran	City council meeting report	Present
4:05	Loren	Schedule adjustments	Discuss
4:10	Jan	First improvement plans	Review and approve
4:20	Ray	New tool: cost-benefit analysis	Present
4:40	Sal	Select next improvements	Cost-benefit analysis
		Closing	
4:55	Terry	Review mission, plan, and action items, plan next agenda, review meeting	Discuss
5:00	Chair	Adjourn	Consensus

Get agendas out well in advance so everyone can prepare. And no matter how proud you are, review your perfect agenda at meeting start.

HOW TO RUN TEAM MEETINGS
(continued)

Group Memory

You might have noticed all the emphasis on writing ideas down on flip-charts. Is this really necessary? Yes, it is. To explain why, let's look at how we remember. When you hear or see something, you record it in your individual memory bank. To remember something, you search your personal "database" to find that piece of information, as this diagram shows . . .

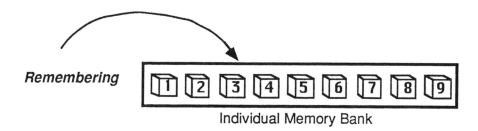

What happens in a group setting? Experts estimate that we listen at about 25 percent efficiency. The following picture shows four team members' individual memory banks that haven't recorded everything that occurred . . .

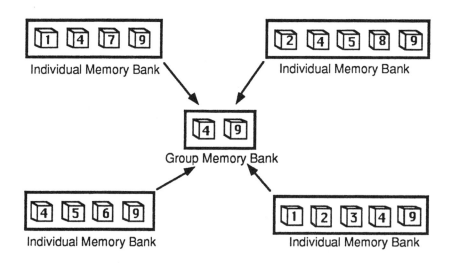

You see, unless a team uses a real-time memory device like a flipchart, they only remember a small part of what actually happened. That's why it's important to create a group memory . . .

COLLECTING DATA

One advantage of teamwork is that it encourages people to open up, speak their minds, and use their full creative powers. But, team decisions should be based on facts, not just private opinions. You need to discuss what's really going on, now just what one or two of you think. To see that emotions and personal agendas don't run the whole show, center your team meetings around data you've collected from stakeholders and experiments.

You'll want to collect and consider two sorts of information . . .

> ► **Hard data**   Facts, events, statistics, procedures, documents

> ► **Soft data**   Opinions, feelings, attitudes, desires, stresses

to help you get a better picture of the problem or process you're trying to improve, track what's actually going on, canvass stakeholders for input, test assumptions, resolve differences of opinion, and make sounder decisions. You can find out how frequently something happens, how serious a problem is, what causes repeating breakdowns, if a new solution works, how satisfied your customers are, and how valuable or scary a particular change would be.

To ground your meetings in reality, collect data by . . .

1. deciding what information you need,

2. selecting the best method to collect the data,

3. all taking a hand in recording the data,

4. analyzing the data collected looking for patterns and trends, and

5. presenting your findings.

Data collection methods you might want to use include observing processes, reviewing statistical reports, posting checksheets for operators to record during work, running experiments, conducting tests, interviewing customers, or holding focus group meetings. Ask your team facilitator about different ways to graph and chart data for easier analysis and presentation.

COLLECTING DATA (continued)

Handling Tangents

A meeting tangent is an off-the-point remark which steers a discussion away from the agenda topic. Tangents occur all the time in new teams. Instead, you want to track or develop the ability to stay on topic without wandering off. Here are a few suggestions to keep focused . . .

- Ask if you're not sure what the topic and process is.

- Gently remind speakers of the agenda item.

- Ask an on-track question to refocus the team on the topic.

- Summarize what's been accomplished on the agenda item so far.

- Suggest that tangents are captured on a bin list for later review.

Another good use of flipcharts is to capture tangents on a page taped on the wall titled *bin list* or *parking lot*. When you hear an off-topic remark, suggest it gets added to the bin. Bin listing is a polite visible way for you to stimulate open communication while staying on track. By having a public place to capture random thoughts and new insights, you'll encourage each other to think innovatively and, at the same time, stay focused.

For more details about running and participating in team meetings, see Marion E. Haynes, *Effective Meeting Skills: A Practical Guide For More Productive Meetings*, Crisp Publications Inc., 1988. Two other valuable tools for improving team communication are *Developing Positive Assertiveness* by Sam R. Lloyd, 1988, and *The Business of Listening* by Diane Bone, 1988, both from Crisp.

CONSENSUS DECISION MAKING

Teamwork requires that all of you pool information and consider different viewpoints to find solutions and make decisions. Yet, the chances are pretty slim that you'll have exactly the same idea about an issue. If you let the most powerful person make the decision or the majority rules, the input of some members will be ignored.

What happens to your motivation when your ideas are immediately rejected? How invested will your teammates feel if their suggestions aren't even considered? Expect that contracting will suffer tremendously. Teamwork may totally collapse.

Instead, make key decisions by consensus. Webster's defines consensus as agreement, especially general opinion. It comes from the word *consent*, the real issue of teamwork. When you make a consensus decision, you've agreed to accept, support and fully act on the choice. Though the selection may not be anyone's first choice, team members must agree that it's workable and that they can live with it. You can't out-argue teammates, get them to give in, and then call it consensus. All members must agree that the decision will work and that they'll go along with it.

Consensus is a decision or position that reflects the collective thinking of a team and that all team members participate in developing, understand fully, can live with, will actively support, and believe is workable.

Since unanimous decisions are rare, most team consensus is an idea that merges the best thinking of all team members. Sometimes one suggestion is accepted as universally best, but most often the team's position combines individual thoughts.

For in-depth coverage of this topic, read *Achieving Consensus* by Eileen Flanigan and Jon Scott. Crisp Publications. 1996.

CONSENSUS DECISION MAKING
(continued)

When To Use It

Many teams can't resist the temptation to use the consensus process exclusively once they've mastered it. This decision-making approach is open and fair, but it's also demanding, time-consuming, and often requires skilled facilitation, especially at the beginning. Should you use it for everything a team does?

You'll probably want to use consensus for important decisions like:

- Your team charter and master plan

- The ground rules you'll follow

- Decisions with major impact on the course of a project

- Final analysis of a problem or resolution of a team conflict

- Commitment to a course of action when collective action is needed

When you don't really care which way to go, you trust a skilled expert. Or if you're deciding details that don't affect the course of history, use another method. This includes majority voting, individual choice, or team leader decision. How long does the whole team need to debate noncritical issues like meeting location, one-to-one differences, or the wording of minutes?

How To Reach Consensus

Flipcharts come in handy when making team decisions because you need the full input of all members while everyone else is listening. To reach consensus, all team members must:

▶ Express themselves clearly and participate fully,

▶ Be open-minded, listen fully, and respect other views,

▶ Respond verbally with acknowledgment and feedback,

▶ Propose solutions to differences and be willing to negotiate, and

▶ Identify areas of natural agreement and actively seek consensus.

Obviously, that leaves out majority voting as a consensus process since it cuts off discussion too soon. Prioritizing by intuition might work, but whose do you follow? You can always compromise or escalate decisions, but this will probably stunt the team's growth and sense of empowerment. Instead, you need to face disagreements and explore solutions until you find a win-win. Everyone must feel that their viewpoint has been heard and that they contributed to the collective outcome.

How can you make this work quickly and effectively? The diamond diagram shows the three phases of communication that you need to move through to make a consensus decision. First, you generate ideas by stimulating discussion, using open questions, and brainstorming **creatively.** The top of the diamond shows that you're trying to pry open minds at this point. When you record all input on charts in full view, **analysis** becomes easier. Get everyone to understand each other's ideas by reviewing what's on the charts. Then group, combine, chart, map, or evaluate all this input. The challenge in the middle of the diamond is to turn the corner toward a conclusion instead of wandering off on tangents. Finally, you make a consensus **decision** by first summarizing, eliminating, and narrowing. When you've distilled a small list, then you figure out how to include everything remaining through ranking, prioritizing, and dreaming up win-win proposals. The bottom of the diamond shows that you've arrived at one point of agreement.

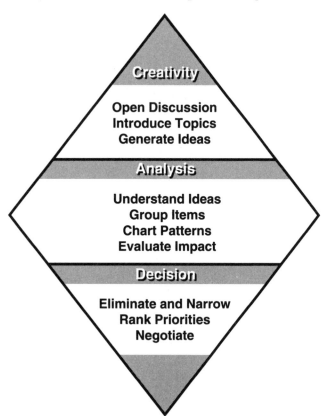

Creativity

Open Discussion
Introduce Topics
Generate Ideas

Analysis

Understand Ideas
Group Items
Chart Patterns
Evaluate Impact

Decision

Eliminate and Narrow
Rank Priorities
Negotiate

CONSENSUS DECISION MAKING
(continued)

CASE STUDY: Team Decision

At the end of road map step two, describe the problem, the Storm Rebuilding Team's list of frequent repairs totaled a whopping 39. Obviously, the city can't afford to fix everything at once so they have to narrow the list to begin step three, identifying the root cause of the problem. It was easy to plan tests for winter damage to downtown streets and the curbs around city hall. Now a major controversy has erupted about storm drains and city parks.

To address the conflict, Terry, the team leader, saw an opportunity to do some just-in-time training with the team. After some outside discussion, the team facilitator, Ray, presented the consensus diamond and briefly explained some of the tools to use at each phase. The team agreed to follow the model to decide which damaged areas could be permanently repaired. Then, Terry took over as meeting chair and led them through the decision process. In a few pages, you'll see which tools they tried at each phase to reach a consensus decision.

 ## Creativity

The first stage of building consensus is applying creativity to stimulate discussion, build participation, generate ideas, and brainstorm lists. You want to suspend your judgement about what you're working on.

Each phase of the diamond has its own set of tools that you need to choose from to fit the situation you're in. Team tools don't look like saws, hammers, and drills. They're specific discussion methods, ways to chart ideas, or techniques to compare opinions. Flipcharts, bin lists, and road maps are examples.

The general tools that the consensus diamond suggests for the creativity phase are:

Open Discussion

Begin conversations by checking in with members and using unregulated conversation to quickly surface reactions.

Introduce Topics

Introduce topics by systematically starting conversations and clearly defining the discussion tool that the team will use.

Generate Ideas

Moderate discussions by asking open-ended questions to build participation and stimulate creative thinking. Get team members to suggest ideas and build on each other's statements without editing, commenting, or judging. Use the brainstorming techniques you learned on page 31.

CONSENSUS DECISION MAKING
(continued)

CASE STUDY: Team Creativity

Terry first suggested that the team openly discuss how much agreement they have about what should be fixed permanently. Five minutes convinced the group to invest more time on this overall subject. Here are their flip-chart notes:

> ### How much agreement do we have about what should be fixed permanently?
>
> Some agreement
>
> Agree on downtown streets
>
> What about schools?
>
> What about parks?
>
> Don't ignore storm drains
>
> Not much agreement

Starting at the top of the diamond, Terry suggested that the discussion moderator lead one cycle of brainstorming.

> ### Which frequently damaged areas should be field-tested to see if they can be permanently fixed?
>
> Downtown streets
>
> Little League fields
>
> Everything
>
> Nothing
>
> Downtown sidewalks
>
> Downtown parking lots
>
> Storm drains near the river
>
> Shopping center parking lots
>
> Streets where we live
>
> School sidewalks
>
> School playgrounds
>
> Garbage route streets
>
> Residential sidewalks
>
> River boardwalk
>
> Residential playgrounds

Analysis

Once you've thoroughly discussed a topic, make sure that everyone clarifies, understands, and values all ideas. Truly hearing each other is typically the weakest part of consensus building. Sometimes inexperienced teams don't document all opinions. Then they try to force a decision before everyone understands what their teammates think and feel. This approach can completely block consensus, convincing the team that they can't succeed, and forcing the team leader to decide unilaterally. The analysis phase prevents this scenario from getting out of hand.

Understand Ideas

There are four ways to better understand what you've brainstormed by getting each of you to carefully consider each other's ideas. You'll almost always want to use at least one of these tools.

Silent Reflection	Quietly read over your lists so you personally think about everyone else's ideas.
Clarification	Identify unclear ideas and then get the original contributors to explain their intent.
Amplification	Ask contributors to go into more detail or have other team members build on each concept.
Buzz Groups	Split up into pairs or subgroups to discuss the ideas on the list.

CONSENSUS DECISION MAKING
(continued)

Group Items

Once everyone says they've fully digested everything on the flipcharts, you can reorganize similar ideas into sets. Grouping isn't always the best next step, but if you can predict it will be, plan to brainstorm with sticky notes that can be easily rearranged.

Affinity Grouping	Move similar items into groups, using post-its or item numbers, and name the sets.
Combination	Identify similar ideas and combine their wording to make composite items.
Categorizing	Identify common themes on the list, name these categories, and then label each item.
Outlining	Organize items into headings and subheadings with items and subitems.

Chart Patterns

Charting, an alternative to grouping, results in a picture, graph, or visual display. It takes a bit more effort than simple grouping, but sometimes it is worth the trouble to clearly show important relationships between your ideas.

Mind Mapping	Graphically draw relationships between items on a chart to show visual connections.
Cause-Effect Diagram	Post items in categories on a cause-effect diagram to show causal relationships.
Pareto Chart	Post data on a stacked bar chart which shows how often an event occurs or how much impact it has.

Evaluate Impact

You can also evaluate the impact or relative value of your ideas. Some of these tools border on decision-making, which is why they reside after turning the corner on the consensus diamond. Use them to compare items so that you're ready to narrow, prioritize, and decide during the next phase.

Impact Analysis	Number items and then list the consequences of each idea one by one on a separate chart.
Pros and Cons	Define the advantages and disadvantages of each item one at a time using a two-column chart.
Cost-Benefit Analysis	Discuss potential costs and benefits or risks and rewards of items to identify relative value.
Forcefield Analysis	Discuss how to minimize and maximize forces driving and restraining a change.

CASE STUDY: Team Analysis

Terry suggested that the discussion moderator check for full understanding by asking if any ideas needed clarification. After a few moment's discussion on several items, everyone seemed clear on what everything meant. Next, Terry suggested categorization.

> ### *Categories*
>
> Downtown   Sports and schools
>
> Non-downtown   River
>
> Facilities

CONSENSUS DECISION MAKING
(continued)

The categories they chose covered everything except *everything* and *nothing*, which they decided to eliminate by common agreement. After labeling all items with the first letter of the category under the discussion moderator's guidance, Mary asked what they had accomplished. A brief open discussion revealed that they understood their options better, but categorizing by location didn't help them decide what should be fixed permanently.

After some thinking, the team decided they needed to order the list two ways to make a decision: by cost of repairs over the last five years, and by frequency of repair during the same period.

Order of Costs ($K)		Order of Frequency	
147	Storm drains near the river	26	Garbage route street
115	Downtown streets	25	Downtown streets
88	Shopping center parking lots	21	Residential sidewalks
71	River boardwalk	17	Streets where we live
67	Garbage route street	12	Downtown sidewalks
66	Residential sidewalks	7	School sidewalks
55	Downtown parking lots	5	Storm drains near the river
34	Little League fields	4	School playgrounds
24	School sidewalks	3	Shopping center parking lots
20	Streets where we live	3	Downtown parking lots
12	Residential playgrounds	3	Residential playgrounds
12	Downtown sidewalks	2	River boardwalk
11	School playgrounds	2	Little League fields

Decision

Most struggling teams complain that their biggest weakness is difficulty in arriving at consensus quickly and easily. In most cases, this trouble can be traced back to little merging of good ideas. This, of course, depends on creativity, flipcharting, and analysis. Yet, even good preparation doesn't guarantee a consensus decision, much less a good one.

Eliminate and Narrow

Of course, your list might have already narrowed while understanding, grouping, charting, or evaluating. If it hasn't, get it down to a manageable size for decision-making using one of these elimination and narrowing tools.

Elimination	Use specific criteria or intuition to remove items that obviously seem impractical or unworkable to everyone.
Multivoting	Ask members to distribute multiple votes to items by raising fingers as the discussion moderator reads down the list or by posting adhesive dots yourself on your charts. By voting for several items or voting several times for your top item, you'll weight priorities to help weed out weak items.
Straw Polling	On each item, ask for a show of hands or thumbs up/sideways/down to determine which ideas to retain and which to discard.

Warning: If you use these tools for final decision-making, you can easily exclude minority views. Use them to determine team member leanings, not to blindly accept the numbers to avoid conflict.

CONSENSUS DECISION MAKING (continued)

Rank Priorities

Next, you will probably want to use one of these tools to rank priorities.

Discussion Ranking	Use open discussion to quickly sort best to worst. Switch to another method if progress is too slow.
Individual Ranking	Using individual ballots or a public scoring chart, post each member's rank of items from best to worst and then add up the scores. Always use high numbers for the top rank so that winning items score highest. When it would take too long to completely rank a long list, simply use a 3, 2, 1 scale.
Pair Comparison	Compare the top two items on the list and, by consensus, reverse the order if the second one ranks higher. Then compare each subsequent pair the same way. Work up and down the list until every item is in the proper relation to each other.
Sequencing	Arrange the items on the list in order of sequence: which should be done first, next, and last.
Decision Matrix	Using a matrix, rank the items in separate columns using different criteria. Rankings can be done by ballot or discussion. Establish final priorities by adding each of the scores from each ranking.

Just because you've prioritized doesn't mean you've reached consensus. Look at the results of any tool, take a moment's open discussion to check what you've learned, and see if a decision is imminent.

Negotiate

If not, use one of these tools to combine the most important ideas and negotiate proposals.

Grouping Tools	Use grouping tools to categorize items or combine the best ideas into a proposal everyone can support.
Trial Balloons	Focus attention on proposing alternatives to bridge the gap between opposing points of view.
Win-Win	Ask team members to come up with new ideas that merge existing options into solutions that satisfy everyone.

CASE STUDY: *Storm Rebuilding Team Decision*

Terry suggested the team first eliminate any damaged area they were sure wouldn't make the cut for field-testing or permanent fixing. A heated discussion broke out about shopping center parking lots. Though they rated third by cost, they were controversial because they really aren't city property. After agreeing upon eliminating some areas, the team came up with 12 items.

> **Which frequently damaged areas should be field-tested to see if they can be permanently fixed?**
>
> Downtown streets   Streets where we live
>
> Little League fields   School sidewalks
>
> Downtown sidewalks   School playgrounds
>
> Downtown parking lots   Garbage route streets
>
> Storm drains near the river   Residential sidewalks
>
> River boardwalk   Residential playground

CONSENSUS DECISION MAKING
(continued)

Ray next taught the team to do multivoting using adhesive dots, issuing five dots to each team member. Here are the results in order of multivotes.

Which frequently damaged areas should be field-tested to see if they can be permanently fixed?

9	Storm drains near the river
8	Downtown streets
5	River boardwalk
5	Little League fields
3	Residential sidewalks
3	Garbage route streets
1	Downtown sidewalks
1	School playgrounds
1	Streets where we live
1	School sidewalks
1	Residential playgrounds
1	Downtown parking lots

Terry then asked the discussion moderator to check what the team thought the dots indicated.

What do the dots mean?

Expensive city repairs are covered

Low frequency items rated low

Little League field ranked high

Schools and playgrounds ranked low

Then a discussion broke out about whether they should field-test all items that received votes or only the top five vote-getters. The team leader, Terry, sat quietly by until a lull in the conversation. Then Terry asked what the budget was for field tests. The team realized they had money to test about half of the items on the list. Quickly the team agreed to test all items that received three or more multivotes.

P A R T

IV

Monitoring
Progress

MONITORING TEAM PROGRESS

Whether your team is working on a project or a continuing job, you still need to manage your work jointly. Project management really means to follow up on your plans, monitor your progress, reinforce what's working, and troubleshoot what isn't. If you don't, someone above you will and you could lose whatever empowerment you started with. That's one reason why you must spend so much time on charters and plans in the beginning. You've already decided what to monitor and how to follow up with sponsor support.

Monitoring is best done by the whole team continuously so that you stay in touch with your position on your plans and schedules. Use monitoring to check your team chemistry to remind each other what needs to be done, and to set up early warnings. It's better to find out early on that your plans need adjustment. Frequent fine-tuning averts crises. By checking routinely, you might also discover what support members need to finish their work.

The three Ps of project management remind you to monitor:

▶ **Plans,** like charter deliverables, master plan milestones, and action plan assignments, to know if you're ahead of, behind, or on schedule.

▶ **Processes** so you're continuously observing how well you're working together, what tools you're using, and how your dynamics are changing.

▶ **Public relations** means paying special attention to how well your communications work with customers, suppliers, and stakeholders.

Pay attention routinely to all three and you'll always know where you are and how to make quick adjustments.

MONITORING TEAM PROGRESS
(continued)

Good Monitoring

The best monitoring is simple, reliable, accurate, and an integral part of work. That way it won't take special effort to stay up-to-date. Here are a few monitoring methods to choose from.

Project board	A timeline diagram that shows major milestones with start and finish targets
Presentation and review	Team members, satellite teams, or the whole team formally present status and answer questions
Regular activity reports	Written progress reports distributed weekly or monthly
Action plan review	Team walkthrough of the status of action assignments on the plan to complete one milestone
Production statistics	Regularly collecting, distributing, posting, and analyzing data about production volume and quality
Budget controls	Regularly collecting, distributing, posting, and analyzing financial data
Work sampling	Conducting quality control spot checks
Operator checksheets	Forms that operators use to record data about routine actions, events, and critical incidents
Dummy run	Walk-through or role play an existing procedure, new process, or action plan to see how it's working
Checklist evaluation and audit	Reviewing a standard list of actions or questions to determine how well things are functioning
Customer satisfaction surveys	Identifying customer perception using written questionnaires or telephone polls
Customer focus group or interviews	Getting feedback from outsiders through one-on-one or group discussions about team progress

CASE STUDY: Team Monitoring

The Storm Rebuilding Team developed a Gantt chart to track their field tests at road map step three.

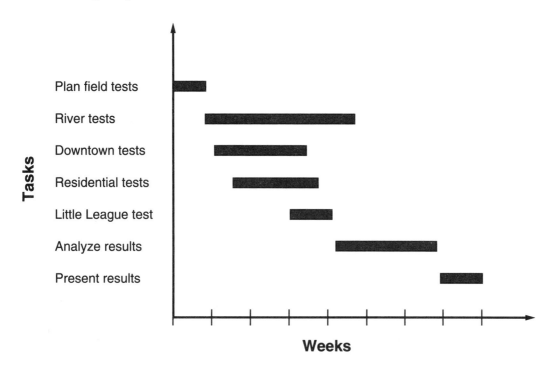

EXERCISE: Personal Monitoring

► Look over your suggested plans for your new team.

► What milestones or actions do you think are really important to monitor?

► What's the best way to monitor these things?

► How closely does your monitoring system match the criteria for a good system: simple, reliable, accurate, and an integral part of the work?

PROJECT MANAGEMENT

Team project management has seven steps. Start with *measurable plans*, keep clear *records, self-monitor* your team's health, *respond* to what you find, maintain good *public relations*, conduct *presentations* as needed, and *wrap-up* properly. Easy, right? Well, maybe not, but at least easy to explain.

#1 Measurable Plans

You already know that to track progress you need to:

- Follow the right road map for your kind of work
- Develop a master plan with a few milestones for each road map step
- Post your master plan on a flipchart at each meeting for a visible reminder
- Break your milestones down into small measurable steps on an action plan
- Update your action plan and road map status at the end of each meeting

#2 Record-Keeping

Record-keeping isn't the most popular team duty. But without it, monitoring suffers. To get support and implement solutions, you need documentation. Team record-keeping includes:

- Translating activities and decisions into official team records
- Maintaining agendas, minutes, plans, statistics, and reports
- Creating reference materials for spreading team findings

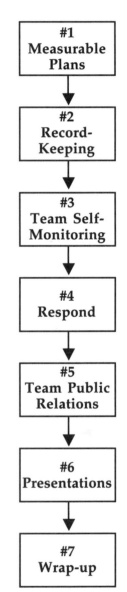

Keeping records will help you focus, keep outsiders informed, confirm commitments, provide reminders, and create a historical database. The tools you'll need include action item register, meeting minutes, and team notebook.

Action Item Register

It's easy to lose track of team activities in the midst of a busy work schedule. Your solution is to track assignments so that you don't forget your responsibilities and commitments. That's why an action item list may be the most important written record you'll ever use.

Action items are tasks that team members agree to complete by a specified time. They record *who* agreed to do *what* by *when.* Action items are the same as a step of an action plan except they come up all the time during meetings. To ensure that action items are completed, your minutes secretary should distribute the list within 24 hours after each meeting. Don't bury the items in the back of your minutes. Instead, put them at the top of the front page.

CASE STUDY: *Team Action Items*

Here's the list that the Storm Rebuilding Team issued after a meeting in the middle of their third road map step.

WHAT	WHO	WHEN
Coordinate Little League field tests with the Park Department.	Chris	July 7
Enter data from river tests into the computer and create a template for future test data.	Sal	July 31
Meet with PSI management one-by-one to solicit ideas about speeding up tests.	Terry	July 1
Review minutes of last two team meetings with team sponsor after vacation.	Pat	July 10
Get previous river studies from the State Water Department.	Mary	July 15

PROJECT MANAGEMENT (continued)

Distributing action item lists after each team meeting is a great idea, but by itself doesn't guarantee that things will get done on time. If you don't review your actions at each team meeting, some may be forgotten. And as you can see from the Storm Rebuilding team's list, some assignments take longer to complete than the time between team meetings. Will anyone remember action items from three meetings ago? To prevent loose ends, use an action register. An action register is a perpetual listing of action items which a team adds to, keeps track of, and checks off when assignments are completed.

To maintain an action register, simply split the *when* column into **date due** and **date complete** columns.

What	Who	Date Due	Date Complete

Instead of issuing a separate action item list after each meeting, add new items to the action register and include a copy with meeting minutes. Review the entire list at each meeting, date those that are done, and adjust target dates or other action items as needed.

Meeting Minutes

Meeting minutes are the journal of team activities. Good minutes are brief, well-organized, readable, self-explanatory, an accurate record of what occurred, and distributed immediately. They help you record your findings, recall your reasoning, reconstruct your thinking, report your problems, and recognize your progress. They take time to compile and read, but they save time by bringing outsiders and missing members up to date.

No matter how important minutes are, that still doesn't mean you'll have lots of volunteers competing for this choice assignment. Unless you're lucky or have someone who is willing to write minutes after each meeting, you'll probably end up rotating the task.

One reason writing minutes is so unpopular is that many teams think they should mimic a court of law or the U.S. Congress. You don't need an unreadable multipage book that documents what happened at a one-hour meeting. Including these items in meeting minutes is usually enough:

- Date and time of meeting plus team members attending

- Major agenda items with any key conclusions and decisions

- Action items or action register

- Date and time of the next meeting with any known agenda items

If you feel the need to elaborate, you could include:

- Reports of action taken between meetings

- Discussion summaries for each agenda item

- Key data or stakeholder input reported

- Informational attachments passed out at the meeting

- Mission statement and road map and master plan position

Just make sure that you don't go overboard. You want to make generating minutes as easy as possible.

CASE STUDY: *Team Minutes*

Why not use the continuous recording of your flipcharted group memory? If your recorder labels each page with the agenda item being discussed and then circles each conclusion or decision, the hard part is done. Just have your minute-taker transfer these items to a form like the **Storm Rebuilding Team Minutes** that follow.

Team	Attendees	Meeting Date
Storm Rebuilding	Fran, Loren, Jan, Ray, Sal	June 20
Agenda Item	**Conclusions and Decisions**	
City council meeting report	Council is happy. Stay in close touch with downtown business representatives.	
Schedule adjustments	Move Little League tests later after the season.	
First work plans	Time-line chart will be published after input included.	
New tool: cost-benefit analysis	Good training.	
Select next improvements	Need to start our homework on residential tests early.	
Who's Responsible	**New Action Items**	**Due Date**
Chris	Coordinate Little League field tests with the Park Department	July 31
Sal	Enter data from river tests into computer and create template for future test data.	July 20
Terry	Meet with PSI management one-by-one to solicit ideas about speeding up tests.	July 1
Pat	Review minutes of last two meetings with the team sponsor after vacation.	July 10
Mary	Get previous river studies from the state Water Department.	July 15
Next Meeting Date: June 27	**Time:** 1:00 pm	**Location:** Room A
Next Agenda Items	Final approval on time-line chart. Review test data template. Report on Little League coordination.	

Team Notebook

To make sure that you keep your records straight from the outset, construct a team notebook. A team notebook is a three-ring binder that contains master copies of all important team documents.

Though you may want one for each team member, a team secretary or historian should maintain the official copy. Here's what you should include.

DIVIDER	CONTENTS
Team Charter	• Team charter versions
Ground Rrules	• Ground rules versions
Plans	• Road map • Long-range master plan • Short-range action plans
Meetings	• Meeting agendas • Meeting minutes • Action items or registers
Data	• Data • Charts • Statistical summaries
Correspondence	• Memos
Reports	• Progress reports • Final reports

PROJECT MANAGEMENT (continued)

#3 Team Self-Monitoring

Though documentation is necessary for project management, paperwork alone won't do much to improve your team's health. To grow quickly through the stages of group development, you'll want to invest a little time in monitoring your team's health by:

- ► Tracking how well you're working together

- ► Raising your awareness of your team dynamics

- ► Learning which team tools work and which don't

- ► Adjusting & refining team ground rules.

If you spend a little time occasionally talking about how you're doing, how you're feeling, and how you could do better, you'll improve continuously. Feedback from trainers, facilitators, and other experts is good too, but if you do it yourselves, you'll progress faster. That's how high-performance teams take charge of their own growth and find their emerging team identity.

So establish checkpoints, solicit open feedback, analyze your performance, and routinely assess changes in your dynamics.

Some self-monitoring techniques include:

- • Reviewing meeting process each time you conclude

- • Receiving feedback from your team facilitator

- • Analyzing meeting minutes for signs of group dynamics

- • Holding team retreats and troubleshooting meetings

- • Having one-on-one discussions outside the meetings

- • Conducting peer performance feedback sessions

- • Regularly using group process checks

Group process checks are a diplomatic way for leaders or facilitators to guide team progress without being bossy. Especially when emotions are rising, someone has to exert a firm, calm hand to defuse tensions. Otherwise the team could do permanent damage to some members' self-esteem.

Group Process Check Method

You can use this simple six-step procedure to call a GPC:

Awareness	A team member or team facilitator observes how a group process or ground rule is working and its effect on your team.
Time-Out	The observer decides the situation warrants change or recognition and calls a group process check by giving the agreed-upon time-out signal ("GPC" or "time-out").
Feedback	The observer quickly explains what was observed with neutral and factual feedback.
Group Process Check	The discussion moderator holds a brief "here and now" meeting so that you can all quickly assess the issue with a moment's open discussion.
Response	If appropriate, you can all suggest solutions and select the best alternative to deal with the situation. You might want to adjust or add to your team ground rules at this point.
Return	Quickly, the discussion moderator should direct you back to the last point of the previous process before the GPC.

PROJECT MANAGEMENT (continued)

Meeting Review

Because meetings are a prime example of how you're doing, meeting reviews are a simple and powerful self-monitoring tool. You just need the discipline to take a couple of minutes at the end of each meeting to check in. You can each fill out a form or use open discussion to determine thoughts and feelings.

For a written review, have everyone fill out a simple form like this:

Meeting Review	Poor				Great
How well did our agenda work?	1	2	3	4	5
How well did we manage time?	1	2	3	4	5
Did everyone participate?	1	2	3	4	5
How open was our discussion?	1	2	3	4	5
How good was our pace?	1	2	3	4	5
Did we get closure on desired results?	1	2	3	4	5

Someone will need to compile the scores so you can discuss the summary at the next meeting.

#4 Respond

Keeping records and monitoring both progress and process isn't any good unless you respond to what you find out. Like any other feedback tool, you have two main actions: supporting and troubleshooting.

Support each other by encouraging teammates. Remember to use positive reinforcement. A team of cheerleaders has more fun and accomplishes more than a team of undertakers.

For example, when you hear good news from stakeholders, pass it on. When a teammate handles something well or solves a problem, make a big deal out of a public announcement. When you've completed an action plan, reached a milestone, or finished a road map step, celebrate. And when someone needs a hand, volunteer. When you find a teammate with less experience than you in a particular job, coach him or her. You'll probably get twice the same support back later when you really need it.

Troubleshoot quickly when monitoring uncovers actual problems. If your early warning system is working, clues will surface about potential troubles before teamwork grinds to a halt. That's the time to stop and take a look. Maybe you'll want to hold a special team meeting to analyze where you got off track, decide how to solve it, and adjust your plans as needed.

For example, treat overdue tasks as problems, investigate what's causing the delay, find solutions, and work around the obstacles. Suggest that team members discuss barriers to project work with their bosses or recruit your team sponsor to help. If you find upset customers, bring them in to a team meeting, calm them down, find out what's bothering them, and decide what you can do to satisfy their needs.

Troubleshooting Tool

Just because you run into an unexpected obstacle in the middle of a project, you shouldn't change your master plan. You might need a short detour, but you don't need to switch to the detailed team problem-solving road map from the planning chapter. To work through a small obstacle, a temporary resource gap, a minor personality conflict, or an unexpected change, you need a narrower approach.

PROJECT MANAGEMENT (continued)

The *Troubleshooting Tool* is a quicker and simpler alternative for this situation. Use these four key problem-solving steps in order by discussing whichever suggested questions best fit . . .

CASE STUDY: *Team Troubleshooting*

Storm Rebuilding Team ran into a little glitch with their river studies. Here's the troubleshooting tool outline they attached to their next minutes.

Problem Description	The State Water Department filed an injunction against the city to stop tests along the river. City officials were upset and PSI management reacted accordingly. At one point, it seemed the team would be closed down. Understandably, we were really frustrated. Giving up at this point would have thrown away any chance of realizing cost savings through permanent repairs after everything we've invested to date.
Cause Analysis	Upon investigation, we found a big misunderstanding at the State Water Department. Somehow they thought we were in conflict with the State's master water plan. After tracing it back, we found neither Dale, our local government liaison, nor Sal, our regulatory agency connection, were in regular contact with them. They each thought the other was covering the representative role.
Solution Decision	We clearly defined that Fran would be the best one to work with the State Water Department hereafter. Dale and Sal were relieved. We brainstormed ways to correct the misunderstanding at the State level and calm our local officials down. The team agreed to convene a joint presentation for the city and PSI after Fran's upcoming meetings in the capitol.
Implementation Plans	Dale and Sal will meet with Fran to debrief what they know about the situation. We will devote 30 minutes at the next regular team meeting to developing an action plan to solve this problem. Fran will present what was covered at the state capitol, and report on how it went. Afterward, the team will plan the local presentation to explain what happened and hopefully how it all got resolved.

#5 Team Public Relations

How many teams run into outside obstacles that prevent them from putting their hard-fought solutions into action? How many great ideas are not implemented just because they weren't communicated persuasively? Don't hoard your good ideas. Instead, develop a network of supporters who help from afar and root for your success.

If you assigned stakeholder representatives during chartering and role definition, you have a good head start on team public relations. Distributing team minutes and staying in touch with customers one-on-one makes good business sense. You'll get valuable input to include into your thinking. You'll find out about related changes while you have time to respond. And you'll surface key objections early enough to solve them.

To monitor how well your public relations is working, ask yourself:

- What information does our sponsor need about progress or problems?
- How can I coordinate regular contact with my assigned stakeholders?
- What written information would interest other stakeholders?
- Are we in close touch with anyone who could veto team decisions?

Use the *Project Reporting Worksheet* to decide what public relations' action to take. Then go through this discussion every few months to monitor how well team public relations is working.

Project Reporting Worksheet

Team Stakeholder Representative	What Should Be Reported?	What Method Of Reporting?	To Which Stakeholder?

PROJECT MANAGEMENT (continued)

#6 Team Presentations

To ensure that your solutions are understood, adjusted, and supported, you need to get skilled at giving interim reports to stakeholders. To get your decisions approved, you must make convincing formal presentations.* If you want your improvements to stick, you need to conduct group training sessions.

POSSIBLE SITUATIONS	POSSIBLE AUDIENCES
Negotiating direction and plans	Team sponsor
Asking for resources and support	Steering council
Collecting data and getting feedback	Customers
Summarizing progress at key milestones	Suppliers
Solving obstacles in the team's way	Other employees
Training others on findings	Industry/community groups
Making final reports	All the above stakeholders

Presentation Preparation

A good presentation has four stages:

1. Opening to warm up,

2. Purpose to focus,

3. Body to present, and

4. Conclusion to wrap up.

---

* For more information about developing your presentation skills, see Steve Mandel, *Effective Presentation Skills,* Crisp Publications Inc. 1987.

Use these steps to fill out the worksheet each time you need to present.

☐ Decide the ideal result you want from the presentation and formulate a statement of purpose to explain it.

☐ Brainstorm topics and anticipate audience questions and put them in order to build an agenda.

☐ Decide on timeframes for each agenda item.

☐ Decide who will present each point or lead each discussion. Be sure you involve as many team members as possible so you demonstrate consensus.

☐ Prepare written agendas, visuals, graphs, handouts, or written reports that will help get your points across and involve the audience.

☐ Plan how to involve the audience with introductions, an opening warm-up, and questions to stimulate feedback.

☐ Arrive early, set up the room, and rehearse if time permits.

CASE STUDY: *Team Presentation Agenda*

Here is the agenda for the local stakeholder presentation that the Storm Rebuilding Team worked out to clear the air about the misunderstanding that occurred with the State Water Department.

Opening	Fran	Introductions
	Jan	Flipchart open discussion: From outside the team, how does it seem Storm Rebuilding is doing?
Purpose	Terry	Review why we're here and meeting agenda
Body	Sal	History and lessons and recent misunderstandings
	Dale	Solutions to recent misunderstandings
	Mary	Master plan status & anticipated cost savings
	Ray	Questions & answers
Conclusion	Fran	Next steps

PROJECT MANAGEMENT (continued)

Completed Staff Work

Many teams are dissatisfied with the amount of power and authority they have. But often the team sponsor doesn't know what's really going on where the work takes place. So why doesn't informing the boss cause some action?

When you update your boss, you create another problem. You've given a busy manager another issue to research, another battle to fight, and another decision to make. Making work for your sponsor can make you unpopular quickly, and it slows down the decision process. How can you take the initiative to solve problems independently?

Completed Staff Work

The best method is a *Completed Staff Work* (CSW) proposal. A CSW is a report that documents your thorough analysis of a situation and a presentation of your proposed strategy. It quickly shows that you've done your research, understand the problem, and know how to fix it. In addition to recommending the best approach, a CSW document and presentation show the alternatives you considered, why you think your solution will work, and how you will implement it.

If the CSW is complete and accurate, the team sponsor doesn't need to start over, launch an investigation, or dream up other options. Since everything is defined, all that's needed is a quick read, a succinct hearing, and ideally, rapid agreement. At least your team sponsor can explain how you can gain quick approval. All of this work dramatically increases your chances of getting to yes.

CSW Contents

CSWs provide a brief review, sponsor confidence, and quick decisions.

Overview	Subject and purpose of document, simple problem label, summary conclusions, your recommendation.
Situation analysis	Description of the situation and need, key facts that define the problem, current data that explains any effects of the problem, relation to organization goals, and a clear statement of the problem's root cause or most basic need.
Recommendation	Clear statement of your proposed solution or decision, why it's the best strategy, benefits to gain, and costs or risks of implementing this recommendation. Include the other options considered and why you rejected them.
Implementation	Action plan to implement the decision, proposed budget and financial analysis, clear statement of what the reader needs to do, what will happen next if approved, and a line for the manager's decision and comments.

Keep your CSW to a page or two for quick reading and presentation. It's better to attach backup documentation rather than clutter the proposal itself. Any documents that need to be reviewed before a decision or issued afterwards should follow. Include reports, spreadsheets, charts, announcement memos, purchase orders, or other vital documents.

PROJECT WRAP-UP

#7 Wrap Up

How often have you found yourself reinventing the wheel? To prevent that from happening to others, you need to document and present what your team did, right and wrong. Yes, this takes time and effort. But it's worth it so others can go forward without wandering around in a wilderness that's already been mapped.

Your first wrap-up task is to develop a **final report** that documents the team's course of action and accomplishments. Compare what you planned with what you did, and objectively evaluate how the team fared. Your report should describe your entire project from beginning to end. Place a checkmark in each box as you complete and include the item.

- [ ] A brief summary

- [ ] The process or problem studied

- [ ] Key data collected

- [ ] Pivotal decisions made

- [ ] Mistakes, obstacles, and solutions

- [ ] Lessons learned and their impact

- [ ] Accomplishments and results

- [ ] Status at the time of completion

If your team maintained a team notebook, compiling a final report shouldn't be an impossible chore. You've already documented your original plan, midstream changes, learning experiences, problems, and solutions.

To prevent past problems from recurring, many teams develop and install a continuing control system before they disband. You're probably in the best position to build and start an early warning system. Also, if you can, turn your final report into training materials so your newfound expertise will never be lost.

The Final Presentation

Next, you should publicly announce successful completion of the project at a **final presentation**. Even though you've been debriefing your team sponsor right up to the end, the big picture often gets lost. Plan a final summary to close out the project. Invite senior management, involved stakeholders, and even external customers. You may get approval to take your show on the road to parade your accomplishments. Sometimes a final presentation gets turned into a training class for anyone who could benefit from what you learned.

Refer to earlier guidelines about effective presentations, and do this one right. You may not want to hire dancers and a band, but do prepare snazzy color visuals and refreshments. Hand out copies of your final report and broadly distribute it as a technical article.

Team Member Closure

This is the time to celebrate overall project completion and recognize all those who contributed. You know that high-performance teams have fun more often than regular people. So make your final bash a party worthy of what you achieved.

If this was your first high-performance team and your work was successful, you've undoubtedly experienced tremendous personal development. Seek out a new position where you can use what you learned. Now that you're an expert in the problem or process you studied, you could contribute as a trainer. Maybe you would like to be the nucleus of another unit that could profit from your expertise. Or maybe you're ready to be a team leader or facilitator. Talk to your boss about your career and next steps. And make sure that your contributions are included in your performance review.

Your final focus should be on the team's redeployment. You built a unit that's worked harder and smarter than a group of individuals could have. Now your charter is complete and you've been successful. It's time to disband the team and move on. But maybe you don't want to break up.

If you want to stay together, you could decide to extend your team charter. All you need to do is convince your team sponsor of the value of continuing. Or you could entirely redo your charter with a new challenge if you can gain management support.

PROJECT WRAP-UP (continued)

CASE STUDY: *Storm Rebuilding Team Wrap Up*

Storm Rebuilding conducted field tests on their top seven priorities and decided that five of them were worth reconstruction during their first year. They got approval for money for all five, crafted a plan for rebuilding, and work commenced. Four of the projects came off as planned. Unfortunately, work on the Little League fields came to a halt when it became a political issue in the mayoral election.

The following spring the team conducted an overall review in preparation for their final report. Team consensus was that, in spite of the Little League field problem, Storm Rebuilding was a great success. The city would recoup its investment within two years, PSI was viewed as a popular partner, and team members grew professionally.

After the final report was presented to a local group of stakeholders, the team held a last meeting followed by a party funded by PSI. All but three of the members enthusiastically volunteered to recharter next year's efforts, solve the Little League problem, and find more savings. After discussion, everyone agreed that a little turnover was healthy, giving others the chance to join in. And those that moved on strongly acknowledged how they developed as a result of their participation.

REVIEW

PERSONAL ACTION PLAN

Review the priorities you set at the beginning of the book.

Which of these did you achieve?

What main benefits did you gain that you think will help your team?

What pitfalls do you especially want to avoid with your team?

What are your plans for working in teams in the future?

NOTES

NOTES

NOTES

NOTES

NOTES

NOTES

NOTES

NOW AVAILABLE FROM CRISP PUBLICATIONS

Books • Videos • CD Roms • Computer-Based Training Products

Subject Areas Include:

Management

Human Resources

Communication Skills

Personal Development

Marketing/Sales

Organizational Development

Customer Service/Quality

Computer Skills

Small Business and Entrepreneurship

Adult Literacy and Learning

Life Planning and Retirement

CRISP WORLDWIDE DISTRIBUTION

English language books are distributed worldwide. Major international distributors include:

ASIA/PACIFIC

Australia/New Zealand: In Learning, PO Box 1051, Springwood QLD, Brisbane, Australia 4127   Tel: 61-7-3-841-2286, Facsimile: 61-7-3-841-1580
ATTN: Messrs. Gordon

Singapore: 85, Genting Lane, Guan Hua Warehouse Bldng #05-01, Singapore 349569   Tel: 65-749-3389, Facsimile: 65-749-1129
ATTN: Evelyn Lee

Japan: Phoenix Associates Co., LTD., Mizuho Bldng. 3-F, 2-12-2, Kami Osaki, Shinagawa-Ku, Tokyo 141   Tel: 81-33-443-7231, Facsimile: 81-33-443-7640
ATTN: Mr. Peter Owans

CANADA

Reid Publishing, Ltd., Box 69559-109 Thomas Street, Oakville, Ontario Canada L6J 7R4.   Tel: (905) 842-4428, Facsimile: (905) 842-9327
ATTN: Mr. Stanley Reid

Trade Book Stores: *Raincoast Books,* 8680 Cambie Street, Vancouver, B.C., V6P 6M9   Tel: (604) 323-7100, Facsimile: (604) 323-2600
ATTN: Order Desk

EUROPEAN UNION

England: *Flex Training,* Ltd. 9-15 Hitchin Street, Baldock, Hertfordshire, SG7 6A, England   Tel: 44-1-46-289-6000, Facsimile: 44-1-46-289-2417
ATTN: Mr. David Willetts

INDIA

Multi-Media HRD, Pvt., Ltd., National House, Tulloch Road, Appolo Bunder, Bombay, India 400-039   Tel: 91-22-204-2281, Facsimile: 91-22-283-6478
ATTN: Messrs. Aggarwal

SOUTH AMERICA

Mexico: *Grupo Editorial Iberoamerica,* Nebraska 199, Col. Napoles, 03810 Mexico, D.F.   Tel: 525-523-0994, Facsimile: 525-543-1173
ATTN: Señor Nicholas Grepe

SOUTH AFRICA

Alternative Books, Unit A3 Micro Industrial Park, Hammer Avenue, Stridom Park, Randburg, 2194 South Africa   Tel: 27-11-792-7730, Facsimile: 27-11-792-7787
ATTN: Mr. Vernon de Haas